Acclaim for Robin Carey

"If *Baja Journey* is a guidebook, so is *A Week on the Concord and Merrimack Rivers*. It goes without saying that I enjoyed it both as a testing-adventure and as a philosophical commentary on man/ nature relationships."

—Wallace Stegner

"Made the mistake of looking at the first couple of pages, then didn't stop till I'd finished the whole thing. A lovely piece of work."

—John Graves

"I read *Baja Journey* twice. An elemental palate cleanser. Quite wonderful, in fact and prose, with occasional tingling Latinate and Elizabethan riffs."

—Jim Harrison

"Reading *North Bank* is almost as much fun as fishing. Carey reports the things so many outdoor writers miss—the things that, when noticed, give fishing joy and meaning and that, when ignored, render it just a 'sport,' like bowling. Forget the 'how to do it.' Here is the feel of a fresh steelhead punching your fly at the end of a run, the music of birds and waterfalls, the fragrance of spring meadows, the colors of canyons when sunlight spills over their rims—the how it was."

—Ted Williams

"*North Bank* joins a small but distinguished group of books, including Roderick Haig-Brown's *Measure of the Year* and Norman Maclean's *A River Runs Through It*, to ponder the connections between one's human and natural community, a home river, and one's beloved pastime."

—Glen Love

"I can't remember when I've enjoyed another angling book so much. Short of Roderick Haig-Brown, I can't think of another Western writer who so effectively and movingly links the active and contemplative sides of fly fishing to a place and its waters."

—*California Fly Fisher*

Upstream

Upstream
Sons, Fathers, and Rivers

Robin Carey

Oregon State University Press
Corvallis

The paper in this book meets the guidelines for permanence and durability of the Committee on Production Guidelines for Book Longevity of the Council on Library Resources and the minimum requirements of the American National Standard for Permanence of Paper for Printed Library Materials Z39.48-1984.

Library of Congress Cataloging-in-Publication Data
Carey, Robin.
　Upstream : sons, fathers, and rivers / by Robin B. Carey.— 1st ed.
　　p. cm.
✓ ISBN-13: 978-0-87071-090-2 (alk. paper)
✓ ISBN-10: 0-87071-090-7 (alk. paper)
　1.　Carey, Robin. 2.　Fathers and sons—United States—Biography.
3.　Kayaking—Klamath River (Or. and Calif.) I. Title.
　HQ755.86.C366 2006
　306.874′20973—dc22

2005035866

Oregon State University Press
500 Kerr Administration
Corvallis OR 97331-2122
541-737-3166 • fax 541-737-3170
http://oregonstate.edu/dept/press

To the memory of those before, and the lives of those after

Contents

Acknowledgments

I am grateful to Catharine, my partner and wife of forty-four years, for her assistance, encouragement, and support; to my son, Dev, for planning a major part of this journey, for sharing his journal, and for maintaining an inspiring faith in the project; also to my daughter, Jennifer, for a gracious understanding of the father-son emphasis in this book.

Tim Palmer and Lisa Jones offered timely encouragement and assistance.

A certain Yurok elder offered his welcome and some good advice.

Wes Chapman drove a marathon shuttle; Karen Chapman sat us down to a magically restorative meal.

Finally, I owe thanks to OSU Press's two anonymous readers for helpful comments and insights.

Upstream

Dad's Camp

Who is the third who walks always beside you?
When I count, there are only you and I together

—T. S. Eliot

We were down at the mouth of the Klamath River where the dunes shift and the river spits itself differently into the sea each month. Bedrock cliffs, standing north and south, gradually disappeared into a fog that rolled in from the Pacific. Wind devils kicked across the spit. Two separate channels of the Klamath braided in from the east through stands of pines. My son, Dev, waved a hand up toward those channels, reminding me that tomorrow we would have to choose between them. We stood at a river access point called Dad's Camp, a primitive RV park near Requa in northern California. Not so many years ago, when I'd driven down to explore the area, there'd been only a snaky double-track through the bushes at this spot, a ripe fish-house at its end, and a concrete boat ramp slanting down to the river. Now a whitewashed building had popped up with an "Office" sign over the front door. A few picnic tables and fire grills dotted the unkempt grass. The boat ramp was still accessible, though its edges slumped, and wide cracks ran across it showing interior rebar. Our kayaks sat unevenly across those cracks as we packed them.

The kayaks were hard-shelled, of classic tapering lines, designed more for covering miles than for playing in waves and holes. Our food, in waterproof bags, we stuffed into the small space between the foot-braces and the forward air bags. Our sleeping gear we stowed behind the seats. In my kayak I had removed the rear support column to make extra storage room, but that space got filled soon enough. We pushed and shoved on our gear, packed and repacked; but it appeared that my day bag would have to fit on my lap under the spray-skirt.

On a nearby riverside bench sat three old men in overalls and T-shirts, patrons of the RV park. They tilted back and looked us over. Wrinkles wove chain-link patterns in their sunburned necks. Their hands stayed carefully stashed in the bibs of their overalls.

"Where you boys headed?" asked one, finally.

"We're headed up," said Dev.

"You boys know what's up there?" asked another.

Dev and I looked at each other. We weren't ready to answer that question. We only smiled, because we knew and we didn't know. The Klamath is a big river. Some sections we knew well; other sections we knew only by reputation. We'd looked at the maps, read some boating literature, talked with some people. A lot would depend on the water level, as always. But exactly what was up there we were going to have to find out first-hand.

The Klamath angles down southwest into California from its headwaters in Oregon, then cuts back northerly to reach the Pacific. In all, it stretches about two-hundred fifty river miles. Over its course the Klamath drops approximately five thousand feet, almost a vertical mile, and there's a feel of that vertical mile in the pressure of its current. Not many rivers have cut their ways through the Cascade Range to the Pacific, but the Klamath managed it, chomping and chewing through hard, igneous formations to get there. The leftovers clutter the river's course down through the canyons. The consequent whitewater attracts boaters from all over the West. Dev and I intended to climb into our kayaks and work up through those whitewater canyons, against the current, against the common direction. The old men on the bench were right to wonder if we knew what we were doing. The going would be slow and difficult. We weren't certain how far we would get.

You might call it the hard way to do things; and if you called it that, you would be guessing close to a deeper cause. Dev and I weren't certain of our motives, but we sensed complexities. Maybe we wanted to look slowly at an experience that can pass too quickly in the downstream mode. We would have to read and judge every boil, every wave, every eddy and micro-eddy, if we wanted to make upstream progress. Maybe we wanted time to consider the mirror of the river and what it could teach us about ourselves. Maybe we wanted to do something hard because there were other things to do between us that were hard, things like cutting past old patterns. Mix in my father's death the previous winter and my need to beat depression from my brain. Mix in my grandfather, a hell-fire frontier preacher and a strap-happy martinet into the bargain, who began, or perhaps continued, a sad generational story of father-son tensions. That gets closer to the bone.

But we had a good feel for the Klamath. Some years back a partner and I had operated a small whitewater outfitting business. Both Dev and my daughter, Jennifer, had worked alongside me as river guides on a number of Oregon and California rivers, but particularly on the Klamath. We regularly ran four different sections of that river, touting our trips in brochures and in boat-show videos. We knew the holes, we knew the waves. Some of the stretches we could have run in the dark of night.

On those trips there were always upstream moments, one guide or another picking a route back up through currents and eddies to retrieve a lost paddle or rescue a stranded client. Conceptually it's not very far from those short upstream pulls to the idea of attempting an entire whitewater river in upstream mode. I used to fantasize about such a trip when Dev was young and impressionable, long before he took to the rivers himself. I had listed sections of various rivers I thought might be challenging but do-able. That wishful thinking laid a foundation for our present plan.

Most people we confided in about our upstream aspirations registered skepticism, however. They thought the idea remarkably crazy. Confronted with such responses, I would recollect an intense young doctor with gunpowder eyes. I'd met him at a CPR class in Medford. He had managed an upstream kayak run of the Rogue River from Illahe to Grave Creek, about thirty-five miles of Class Three water. He and his boating partner had roped through sections of Mule Creek Canyon. I thought that doctor eminently sane. Later I spoke with the partner. He told me the upstream paddling on that trip was incredibly exhausting, but also one of the most rewarding things he'd done in his life.

There was some precedent for our effort, then, and a few like-minded people. If our motives weren't perfectly clear, that was all right with us. If the outcomes weren't certain, that was as it should be. We didn't need certainties just to don our river shirts and tightly roll the tops of our waterproof bags. Time would deal with outcomes, as it always did. Meanwhile, we went about our preparations. Journeys begin in homely ways like that. You pull on your river shoes. You smell the faintly sour scent of your life jacket. You make sure the Blue Water rescue rope is coiled and handy. And you wonder, on the other side of your mind, if you really are doing what it appears you are doing.

With the packing finished, our river gear donned, a last check made of the necessities, Dev and I waded out into the Klamath and sat back into our kayaks. The meager back supports dug into our kidneys. A tidewater current sucked beneath the hulls. Catharine, my wife, snapped pictures with a black rangefinder and climbed into the Toyota that had brought us down to that place. My stomach dipped as the car pulled away, that last support system leaving. But I managed a cheery wave to Catharine as she drove off. We spun our kayaks. Fog layered and moved along the shoreline. It was evening, and western light shafted obliquely through the murk.

A flock of terns, rasping and purring, circled overhead. Dev and I paddled across a wide lagoon. The western shore, a long peninsular spit, looked too low and exposed for camping. We followed along its interior curve. Off to the north the fog had lifted. Headlands loomed there, and out from them stood a monolithic haystack called North Oregos. We could hear waves pounding against it as we paddled and see spray lifting along its base. Where the far river channel turned upstream and east, a cove tucked itself against a rock face. Its beach appeared friendly, though the pea-stones had blackened from mist. The smoothest expanse of it lay close to the water, just above the weed-line signature of high tide. We landed there, spread out our tarp on the stones, and rolled out the sleeping bags.

We hadn't said much to each other in the crossing, nor there on the beach either. Except for the distant crash of surf, the river lay wrapped in the stillness of drifting fog. Dev had wandered a short way up the shoreline. I was considering some plants behind where the tarp lay spread. A shout startled me—a guttural, wordless outburst of sound, followed by another, that boomed across the shingle, rebounded from the cliffs behind me, and flooded the air with reverberations. It was Dev letting loose.

He looked my way a little sheepishly. "It's good to get back to a river," he said.

I understood that rawboned feeling of freedom in him, and the need to give vent to it, in fact had something of the same feeling in myself, though damped down a level by uncertainties. Dev had been off at Berkeley for some years, then at the University of Arizona. He had known the dried-up brain, the bleary midnight hours, the rough-and-tumble stresses of graduate study. The antithesis of all that was a river canyon, a kayak, and a month of free time.

Dev ambled down to the kayaks and began repacking gear. I sat cross-legged on the tarp. Out beyond the spit to the south stood another haystack monolith, South Oregos, jutting and ponderous, the crest of it sheening in evening light. I studied it and recalled what I had read—the Yuroks used to paddle out to South Oregos in their ocean-going dugouts, beat on the sides of the monolith with sticks to get its attention, then pray to it for good salmon harvests. While I studied South Oregos, two river otters swam up close to our camp, looking things over, then dove. A great blue heron soared toward us, squawked in surprise, flapped, lifted, and opted for an adjoining bay. A killdeer tilted its wings along the water's edge. Dev said, with a grin, "They're supposed to be on golf courses."

Our brains began clicking incrementally into journey mode. We occupied ourselves with small chores and short forays. I noted from a distance what a world of blue we'd gathered to ourselves—one kayak, one paddle-shaft, one helmet, one sleeping bag, one wind jacket, both life jackets, both spray skirts, all the river bags, and that eight-by-ten tarp. The western horizon kept darkening, and soon we settled down for the night. With my sleeping bag smoothed, and a hip-hole dug out in the pebbles, I felt comfortable enough. Dev, beside me, checked constellations as they brightened into view. We took deep breaths of the sea-smelling air. We had begun. We had braved the nay-saying opinions, passed beyond the old men of Dad's Camp, and crossed to an opposite shore. Everything from that moment forward had a point of reference and a place in the river's time.

ᕦ

Vaguely uncomfortable, I awoke in the night. Dev had worked deep into his sleeping bag and lay curled on the tarp like a great caterpillar. The stars glinted on the river. Across the river a single night-light shone at the office building of Dad's Camp. The eminent ethnologist Alfred Kroeber had visited the Yuroks down here at the mouth of the Klamath, at the Yurok village of Rekwoi (Kroeber's spelling). He'd gathered data on Yurok customs and myths, recording, among other things, the Yurok belief in diminutive spirit ancestors of the tribe. These tiny people, called *woges*, frequented the landscape, hiding themselves in trees and in stones. The Yuroks are an Algonkin people, and it might be that these spirit ancestors represent a racial memory of origins. Nobody really knows. But I liked the idea of a people, pint-sized, hiding in rocks and trees, coming out at night the way Kroeber says *woges* do. Sometimes they frightened children, who would see them at dusk; and then a grandmother of the tribe would go out to where the *woges* had been seen, shake a stick, and sing her song of protection: "Go on away, leave the children alone, do not bother us."

I'd been thinking some of my own ancestors, partly because of bad dreams I'd been having about my father. My depression following his death seemed unnaturally intense and prolonged. This was more baggage on a trip already tight with baggage. Many nights in the previous months I'd awakened with tears running down my face. I concluded that fathers die, but they don't necessarily leave. Also, certain patterns of my family unsettled me, and they traced back toward my paternal grandfather, Thomas— not simply, not solely, but largely. It occurred to me that Thomas was a kind of *woge*, diminutive and bothersome, frozen in my mental landscape, and that my protective grandmothers were long gone. Maybe I could visit Thomas the way the Yuroks visited South Oregos, paddle in hand. Maybe I could paddle up to the lineage of fathers and pound out some understanding of my own rearing, and of that whole linkage of paternal influence running from Newcastle, England, where my grandfather was reared, through Scott City, Kansas and various Podunks of Indian Territory, where my father took his imprint, and then on to my own involvement in the line.

As I lay there on that Klamath beach, thoughts of my father rattled in my brain like dried peas. I recalled how he had spoken to me of chess, Ping-Pong, Montana agates, and the Christian life. But he'd never said much that was personal, and certainly not much about his brutal upbringing in the Territory. I closed my eyes and reviewed the familiar, post-stroke image of my father's brain on the CAT scan. A cluster of cells along one side had gone dark and blurry, as though a fog had rolled right through his cranial bones.

I slept again, and woke again, this time in early morning, my hips achy. Beaded dew covered our sleeping bags. Propped up on one elbow, I noted the moon's hazy glow above a fog-mass. High-tide water ran down through the sand of the beach, miniature rivers seeking the least resistance, sensible and gravity-abiding.

Dev stirred and rolled over. "Listen!" he said. "Hear it?"

I listened to a clear whistle followed by spiraling updrafts of notes.

"Swainson's thrush," said Dev. "That's a good omen."

The air was nippy and the bags warm. We lay back to let the dawn brighten. The thrush kept fluting. But we were eager to begin, and soon crawled out of our bags. We pulled into our clammy river clothes. Some handfuls of granola sufficed for breakfast. We stuffed our damp sleeping bags, carefully repacked the kayaks, and pushed out into the river. I harbored a comic-book image of our paddling vertically up the side of a mile-high skyscraper, hanging up there against girders and glass like two fusiform spiders. I smiled at the thought, and Dev, glancing at me, knew at least that my mood was good. We were as ready as we would ever be. In our kayaks we had river-rope, pulleys, Prusik cords, and carabiners.

We jostled our kayaks in the dark water, getting the balance and the feel of them. I intoned, jokingly, "Three herons past a full moon, in the year of the river, our journey began."

Dev laughed. "Better write it down."

We paddled southwest, out to the river mouth, so as to begin at the absolute beginning, a fine point, certainly, but an important one to Dev. Surf pounded, and masses of seals slid down into the river from a sandbar. Their heads bobbed up around us, baleful eyes watching us from every direction, the smell of them strong in the air. We stopped paddling and absorbed the scene. Pinks and yellows flared across the western sky, the Pacific glimmering in morning light, the seals bobbing around us like so many marker buoys. Terns dipped overhead. Then a human voice pierced across the dunes.

"Watch out for the rip!"

We saw the fisherman shouting at us from a southern promontory of shoreline, waving his hands. The river suddenly tilted beneath us, roiling and pouring at a powerful angle down toward the surf. We had carelessly floated past the lip of the drop. Looked at one way, it was a good start to our journey, forcing an uphill mode from the outset. Maybe I yelled at Dev too abruptly, and pulled with my paddle harder than necessary. Dev was nonchalant about it all. "It's only surf," he said, paddling to stay even with the drop.

We pulled hard, working back up over the lip and into a calmer section of river. I paused, catching my breath, and fixed an eye on Dev. "There are rash young adventurers," I puffed; "and there are careful old adventurers; but there are very few rash old adventurers." I smiled crookedly when I said this, savoring the aptness. But it was the father-stuff getting started, too, before we had fairly begun.

Dev said, "Surf's no problem. We could paddle out through it if we had to. And then back in again."

Feeling his push against my imagined authority, I steadied myself. It was all natural enough. I remembered feelings for my own father, how my stomach balled up whenever I drove back to visit him in Wisconsin, how my eyelids developed tics that popped and jumped in his presence. Even after his stroke, I felt nervous around him. One day in the hospital room, his catheter paining him, he shouted out, "Crap!" Despite his stroke-impaired speech, that word found its way unobstructed from his brain to his tongue. Hearing that word, I felt my stomach drop. Sweat broke out on my head. *Crap* was the plague-word of my youth, a judgment fired regularly in my direction. His word echoed off the septic walls, hovered over the tubes and the bed sheets, and I felt again like a failed and worthless teenager.

Outside in, or inside out, feelings of failure and worthlessness get ugly. I am just beginning to understand my father's autocratic ways in that light, just beginning to realize how often he stood before his own father, Thomas, feeling failed and worthless, and, at the same time, absorbing that parental model of the judge.

An incoming tide flowed with us as we started upstream, and a wind blew at our backs all the way to the Highway 101 bridge. Orange spray paint spelled out a gaudy "Y-u-r-o-k" on a mid-river pier, but the golden bears above us, guarding both ends of the bridge, glinted nicely in the sun. The wind stayed with us to Klamath Glen where a Kiewit Pacific gravel mill churned and rattled, conveyor belts clanking under clouds of dust. Two women swimming in the river with their children asked us how far upstream we were headed.

"As far as we can get," I said.

The women looked at each other, laughed, and shook their heads.

A Yurok presence further announced itself with gillnets staked on gravel bars, but otherwise the Klamath appeared unpeopled. Riverbanks stood quiet and shaded with black oak, tanoak, and fir. The river's surface looked open and bright, the way I wanted to feel. Long pools held unriffled at the bends, and the paddling was easy.

Past the pools, though, we encountered graveled pour-offs, no eddies to work, no boulders to hide behind, just downstream push. We jumped out and waded these, water mounding against our shins. The ropes I'd rigged to the kayaks worked well enough for towing, one end tied to a stem loop, the other snugged into a back-deck cleat. We could jump out and grab a rope in one motion. We walked a number of pour-offs that afternoon. The kayaks nosed behind us like leashed hounds.

"Let's forget miles and count walk-ups," I said.

"Let's forget miles and count nothing at all," said Dev.

Clearing a river bend, we saw ahead a wide rapids with a steep drop. Logs and debris created wicked-looking blockages along both sides. Below the center drop, a shallows glowed yellow-green under the white churn. We jumped out there, in the center of the river, waist-deep in current, and pushed our ways up around boulders with the kayaks in tow. Ahead of us the upstream bottom sheered down and away, too deep for wading. Behind us the drop sucked and bounced insistently under the kayaks. Dev ran a reckless calculation of odds, managed an upstream shove of his kayak, and made a flying entry, his six-foot-six-inch frame a help, his kayak's key-hole cockpit a help for a quick tuck-in of legs. I myself, slithering and clawing, made no headway. Dev paddled back, latched onto my kayak with his clip-rope, and towed while I hung on behind.

"First rescue," he announced, laughing and obviously pleased by the challenge. Undoubtedly pleased, too, by the hot sun on his back and the pounding blood in his youthful heart. I looked back at those weirs of logs, brush, and boulders below me in the river, and was glad enough to be past them, whatever the method.

We paddled on, Dev moving out ahead; but first-day aches tested us both. We had lost the tidal push and the upstream winds. Back muscles and stomach muscles cramped from holding ourselves stiff and upright. It began to be hard, hurtful work. When we could, in rare places of slack water, we bent out over the front decks of the kayaks, wrapped our arms around the hulls, and stretched our backs.

After a good many hours of paddling, and what I guessed to be about ten miles of upstream progress, with evening coming on, we pulled ashore to a high north gravel bar covered with ragweed. We carried our kayaks far back from the river. One relatively open spot accommodated the tarp. With our packs at the edges of the tarp, our sleeping bags in the center, opened up to dry, we had a kind of home ground, an established place. We rested there, scrunching our river duffels under our heads, our aching backs supported by firm ground. Our bent knees did not align, Dev's being knobbier and higher off the ground. We found this anomaly amusing, and the amusement further leavened our spirits. We were pleased with our progress. Some of our misgivings had gotten sweated out of us. Excepting the first surf-threatened moments of the day, we had worked in accord, and felt reassured by that fact.

We weren't eager to rise up from our rest, but neither did we want to clean dishes in the dark. We set about dinner chores. Dev had planned the food, no easy thing. My first idea about this trip had been to run a supply-laden car along the river, parking it ahead of us each day or two, using a bicycle for the shuttles. Dev, more of a purist in these matters, had won me over to a simpler plan. We agreed to do without the car, to carry what we could in our kayaks and use river caches, one buried near the Dillan Creek Bridge some miles above Somes Bar, one at Thompson Creek Lodge above Happy Camp, and one at the Copco Reservoir store near the Oregon border. On our drive to drop the caches we had checked other stores along the route, their hours, and what kinds of produce they carried: Headway Market in Happy Camp, the Rainbow Store in Hamburg, Quigley's in Klamath River. We'd jotted down locations of public phones and mailboxes: Clear Creek, Seied Valley—places spaced out in thirty-, forty-, fifty-mile hops.

At Thompson Creek Lodge, a regular overnight stop for us in the outfitting years, the stolid-faced woman who had answered our knock and our query, said, "Charlie Polk? Charlie Polk moved back to Kansas."

She'd taken our cache, anyway, said we could leave it on the porch and she'd take care of it later. She'd kept her screen-door closed, opening it finally just a hair to hand me her business card with the phone number on it. Evidently, she didn't trust our looks.

I couldn't help but think she was seeing us at our best, too. Next time, if things went as planned, we'd be crusted and bearded river-pilgrims. And Kansas, I thought, Charlie Polk, our old host of the river, gone back to Kansas, to the sod-hovel homeland where my own father was born.

On our Klamath gravel bar, a blue flame burned in the camp stove beside the tarp. Dev dropped pasta into the boiling water with aplomb. Judging from contents of the duffels, I figured we'd be eating a lot of pasta. Pasta was a good choice, I allowed, compact and nutritious. I sat drinking iodized water from a bottle and entertaining puerile hunger fantasies. Dev drained the pasta and sprinkled it with basil. We forked it into our mouths in big lumps and drank more water. Afterwards, we washed dishes together down at the shore, scraping them clean with sand.

Dev and I had agreed to keep separate trip logs. We got these out, sat cross-legged on the tarp, and wrote. Mine was a hard-bound one given to me by Dev as a pre-trip gift. He had added a cover of thick paper and ink-sketched the front with a map of the Klamath River showing various mountain landmarks of the drainage. On the back he'd fashioned the names of Klamath rapids into a spiraled line, each letter of each name making a small section of the course. I was touched by the gift, touched by his eagerness to do the food, touched by his enthusiasm for this shared time.

That log had a special place in my river pack, protected by a plastic bag. The selfsame log has a special place beside me now, months later, on my desk. Its cover is warped and stained by Klamath water. Its pages hold the words and hold the sketches. Its pages hold various pressed flowers and a couple of feathers. I read it repeatedly for some clue of purpose, some affirmation of relationship. We never expected miracles, Dev and I. Relationship can set up as unbending as river canyon. But in the interstices the water keeps working. In the bedrock the pebbles turn. I search through this log of mine now for something like that, some small erosion of old pattern. I sense something there, rolling along under our overt talk and action like flakes on the river bottom, something difficult to name, something hard to scoop up, hard to extract.

ᔕ

Early the next morning, fog still hanging along the banks of the river and the sun not yet risen, a small motorboat passed our campsite headed upstream, the two people in it scanning the shoreline. Dev and I lay motionless in our sleeping bags, hidden in the ragweed.

"They don't see us."

"No."

We shared a clandestine moment as we hunkered there outside the pale of sensible endeavor. When the distant drone of the motor had faded, we crawled out of our bags, ate granola from our cupped hands, pulled on our wet clothes, shivered a little, stuffed our gear, and hurried to our kayaks knowing the paddling would warm us. We set off, rounded a few bends, and discovered a large creek flowing into the Klamath from a north canyon, Blue Creek according to our map. The motorboat we had seen earlier was pulled ashore there. A man and woman fly-fished the confluence riffle. To my inquiry the woman answered that she'd hooked a couple of small steelhead, "half-pounders," but that in relative terms the fishing was slow. I asked her how far it was to Weitchpec. Dev grimaced at my question, a counting question, a gotta-get-there question. The woman laughed and said, "Quite a ways yet to Weitchpec." Dev was right about my intention, too. I had told Catharine I would try to call her from Weitchpec, that we should make it there in three days, maybe four days of paddling. I had it in mind to be on schedule.

The Klamath grew more brawny and wild with each mile we paddled. We had reached that section where the only road, the north-side road from Pecwan to Klamath Glen, never much of a road to begin with, had washed out some years before and stayed that way, no passage through now to Highway 96, or from it, meaning that a river shuttle for this section had to run all the way down to Arcata and then up the coast. This was a hard stretch of river to reach, and it felt that way, felt remote, primitive, not much changed at all from the time when Jedediah Smith and his party, driving some three hundred horses, their *caballada,* had wandered in circles along these ridges trying to find a way to the Pacific, the natives alternately feeding Smith's party and threatening them, Smith alternately accepting food and shooting recalcitrants. Smith, in his journal, referred to the Klamath as the "Indian Scalp River."

Dev and I had never run this section of canyon, those shuttle logistics being the main reason; and we marveled at what we had missed—clean water, old-growth forest, a landscape about as untouched physically as any remaining place in the West. An 1855 treaty had set this section apart for the Yuroks, and it was salutary to see that the Great White Father had managed a decent outcome here, for a time at least, despite various boundary squabbles and gold-venture probes. Now, of course, a water dispute rages with Klamath Basin farmers, and salmon are dying in unprecedented and untoward numbers.

This lower section of the Klamath, despite its primitive beauty, had a bad reputation in boating circles—tire-slashings at the put-ins and take-outs, rock-lobbings and pot-shot parties along the corridor. A month previous to our trip I'd called the Forest Service station at Orleans to discuss our plans. I'd asked the ranger on the line about the current political climate and if we should anticipate problems with the Yuroks. He'd paused for a moment, then said, "How lucky do you feel?"

Subsequently I'd made a phone call to a Yurok tribal leader. He acknowledged the occasional "hardhead," and politely suggested that we travel "quietly." It appeared the world was full enough of worrisome things, if Dev and I wanted to worry about them; but the Klamath itself, as we paddled along, appeared almost deserted. We saw occasional boats drawn up on sandbars, but few other signs of people. We were seen several times, probably more often than we knew; but we were not bothered in any way. Whether that tribal leader had put in a word for us, or whether the Yuroks chose to respect our upstream quest, or whether we were just lucky, I couldn't say.

Gradually we were leaving behind us the alluvial riverbed of the delta and moving farther up into the bedrock of the coastal range, and of that north- side cross-range called the Siskiyous. (I'd lived thirty-odd years at the base of the Siskiyous and only recently learned that the name is French: *Six cailloux*—six stones— supposedly marking a crossing on the Umpqua River to the north.) Dev and I started to assess river current and to calculate new ways of dealing with its force. Dev talked about flow, how the river flowed over itself, how the current slowed along the edges of the river, and along the bottom, and in areas of turbulence—places of laminar friction. When we couldn't find upstream eddies, we looked for sections of shallow chop, finding it easier to paddle there.

"Why does increased volume mean increased velocity?" I asked, and we laughed because it was an old question, discussed on many a downstream trip.

"What was the guy's name who worked that out?"

"Bernoulli," said Dev.

I suspected this laminar complexity must work also in the blood, occlusions slowing down my flow, all those clean, supple young vessels of Dev's speeding things up, no chop to his system, no wasted turbulence to his energy. Something must explain the distance he kept putting between us, his upstream speed. Too, he was faster getting into his kayak, and getting out. He perfected an entry technique, starting with the kayak pointed downstream, letting the weighting and the current turn it upstream as he swung his legs in and tucked his feet. He got fast and smooth with the method.

"Tao," he said laconically. "Use the natural laws."

His words seemed grounded in fundamental knowledge, but they also sounded distant to me, the words of a stranger. He seemed so mature, suddenly, his black beard thickening, his forearms swelling with muscle and veins, his confidence evident—so like those otherworldly daredevils I'd met in commercial river circles, guides just returned from the Bio Bio, or from Nepal, those nut-brown boy-men grown friendly with death and cataclysm. It all made me aware of how long Dev had been off at school, of the intervening years.

Each time Dev got ahead, he'd stop and wait for me. His stiff new fuchsia kayak was faster than my warped old blue kayak, of that I was certain; but our disparity of speeds came from something more than that, some lethargy that grew in my arms as each day progressed. I had always been strong with a paddle. The slogging pace I was managing disturbed and annoyed me. Dev humored me along saying this was marathon-mode; slow and steady was appropriate.

Emotions circled in me like a do-si-do, and I realized that my intermittent depression was an issue of this Klamath journey. Depression didn't match up well with intrepid spirit. It tended to sap energy and undercut perseverance. I shook my head, and shook it again, trying to clear it, morbid images buzzing around me like wasps, thoughts of what I should have done about my father, guilt at not having been there at the end, recollections of my father's crumpled body. I wished I could brush those thoughts away. But my father was everywhere I looked—down in the bedrock, mixed in the evening light, mixed with the shifts of this river's moods, mixed with the lethargy in my arms. I recalled the debilities of his stroke, his flesh altered to useless stuff, and his groping attempts to answer simple questions put to him by eager and always-youthful therapists.

"What color is this, Reverend Carey?" they would ask, holding up a bright green placard. Unable to speak the word, my father would start to hum "When Irish Eyes Are Smiling." But a tune was a response not on the charts, not in the training. "No, No,

No," they'd say. "What *color?*" And there it was again, that language gap between the generations, that space between the hearts, that occlusion in the words.

I remembered his blue-veined, still-sinewy legs, the legs of a high jumper and middle-distance runner. He'd used the old scissors style of jumping, the only practical style back in those days when you came down as far as you went up and landed hard in a pit of sawdust. He'd had those springy legs of his still working at the hospital that day I first untied the gauze restraints on his wrists and undid the Posey vest the nurses had put on him. He had rolled out of the bed and set off for the bathroom with so much strength and speed that I could not hold him, could only grab the IV stand and roll it after him, watching blood dribbling down his forearm. Then where did those legs go? No one could explain it to me. He'd lost them somehow. Within two days he could not even lift his feet to the foot-rests of his wheelchair. I thought about that as the Klamath pushed at me, shaped my inner space to its own terms, nothing static any longer, or unchanging, always the backward wash, the perpetual downflow.

We paddled hard and long. Toward evening we reached Pecwan Ridge and the Yurok town of Pecwan, where swimming copper-skinned girls chased after us, splashing and diving like dolphins, shouting and laughing. One grabbed the back loop of my kayak and held on to it, waving to her friends as I towed her along. The town itself showed a small-steepled white church, a square building with a bell that looked to be the schoolhouse, and a few dottings of houses. We worked up past the town, waved farewell to the swimmers, turned a bend, and kept paddling.

Not far upstream from the town, Pecwan Creek came tumbling into the Klamath from the north, traversed by a small bridge; and across from there my shoulders and arms gave out, which accounts for how we stopped at a gravel bar within view of two houses. Dev was not thrilled by the public spot, but he could see my exhaustion. There was sand beach to be had, but we threw down the tarp on gravel, knowing that sand was no softer, and that it would stick to our wet clothes and sneak its gritty presence into our food.

Dev cooked up pasta. We split a green pepper and an orange. Dev sprinkled cayenne pepper on his pasta, then drank a lot of water. We both drank a lot of water, every drop we had. We stumbled back down to the river and filled all the bottles, dripped in the purifier, capped them up. It was a ceremony we enjoyed, one of us holding the bottles, one of us dispensing the iodine drops.

Dev asked about the bruises on my head. They turned out to be blotches sunburned on my scalp through the vent-holes of the river-helmet. There were genuine bruises on my feet, however, the insteps puffy from stumbling over stones. Other bruises had blued up my hips from slamming down into hard edges of the kayak with desperation entries. Then, too, the pre-trip spider bite on my shin had turned milky and soft from the day's soaking, my own little fiefdom of dissolving flesh. I swallowed down my antibiotic dose for that, and watched mares'-tails hanging to the east, and thunderclouds blowing up from the south with a promise of rain.

It was time to let the flesh drift down into dream, the muscles still jerking to impulses of the day's paddling, and I scraped out a hole under the tarp, laid the tarp back down, and swiveled my hips around to find the place, settled down into that form, and let the muscles loosen. The flesh had had its moments, had paddled hard and fended off disasters, had pulled and pushed upstream for some odd miles, but still I didn't trust it. Vague genetic currents ran through it; vague conditioned urges and male compulsions laminated its blood. It held those emotions I could not always control, but felt compelled to control. It blotched in the sun.

It was flesh of my fathers, and back there, in their lives, lay some serious bruises, psychic bruises, not just bruises to the feet, not just blotches on the head. I needed to pay some attention to those, I realized, gather what I remembered and what I could search out, and put it all together. Because somehow those bruises had worked forward to my own life, and without knowing certainly just how or why, I knew I felt them. If I was ever going to understand my current depression and my nightmares, get past those roadblocks and on to better places, particularly with Dev, I needed to look at those old bruises of my father's, go back to the *woges* and work out some understanding, get down to the bedrock bottom of things.

"Goodnight, Dev," I said from inside my sleeping bag.

"Goodnight, Dad."

Thunder and lightning arrived soon enough, the moon looking almost eclipsed as cloud-masses crossed it. I stumbled up to move gear around so that I could fold the tarp over Dev and myself the instant the rain started. I lifted gear and pushed gear, then scrabbled around trying to relocate my hip-hole under the tarp. Dev woke up. We lay there with our eyes open for a long time, waiting for rain.

Rain

My father's father, his father's father, his—
Shadows like winds.

—Wallace Stevens

My father's jumbled study held some notes he'd made about his early life with Thomas. He'd put the notebooks under his wooden pipe stand for safe-keeping. Various pipe stems, chewed and stained, pointed down at the notes like crooked fingers. The recollections were random, disorganized, handwritten, some pages holding no more than a word or phrase, but they held some answers about paternal legacy. I had heard the odd reference, vague and fleeting. The notes amplified and solidified my impressions. The facts weren't pleasant, but they made my father more understandable. Two years previous he had named me executor of his will and directed me to his study for whatever information I needed. He must have known I would find those notes.

At the time I discovered them, my father was in West Allis Memorial Hospital in Milwaukee. I'd flown out from Oregon when I'd gotten word of his stroke. It was late summer, and late evening. I had just come off a three-day guiding trip on the Rogue River, and my mind was full of eddying currents and river sun. All that changed. One of my father's friends picked me up at Billy Mitchell Airport and drove me to the hospital for a look at my father, his false teeth perched on his bedstand like the smile of the Cheshire Cat. He was sleeping, so we left and drove down to my father's red-brick house on 65th where I would spend the night. The house was a midden. The closets swelled with junk and boxes that sloped from the floor to the ceiling like heaps of slag. Dirty dishes mounded in the sink. Mold bloomed on a kitchen rug. It had all gotten away from him at the end. I wished I had known. I remembered that exhausted voice of his on the telephone and knew I should have known.

I crawled into my father's bed, but couldn't sleep. It felt strange to be lying in his bed, contouring my own hips to the declivities of his mattress, and there were things to be done. There were resources to gather and a rescue to organize and implement. I dressed again and made some coffee. That's when I found the notes. I took them immediately to my father's chair, under his reading lamp, and sat absorbed in them well into the morning. Baleful relatives stared down at me from the walls while I read, and rain rattled against the windows. The notes laid it all out, the sordid history of things, clear, but far away and long ago.

My father's mother, Addie, a Kansas schoolmarm, died of puerperal fever. I have found an old photograph of Addie looking down the barrel of a photographer's rifle, and her dark eyes shine with fun. Had she lived, she might have lifted my grandfather's mind out of its habitual severity. Maybe opposing dispositions explained the attraction between them. Hers was a Boston family, the Longs. She was one of twelve children and the second Addie, the first Addie having died young. For uncertain reasons, presumably for a teaching position, she ended up riding the Atchison, Topeka, and Santa Fe to western Kansas in 1899 or thereabouts, only twenty-odd years after Dull Knife and his Northern Cheyenne had passed through.

Kansas school-teachers of that time were almost all women. The salaries were low, about twenty dollars a month for the best positions. Most of the teachers boarded out, rotating from family to family of the students they taught. Schoolhouses were small and smaller, smelling of coal smoke, many with dirt floors. Students drew their math equations in the dirt with pointed sticks. Books were few. Webster's blue-backed speller was a standard, as was the McGuffey series of hero tales illustrated by Henry F. Farny. Many students brought Bibles or almanacs from home as their readers. Benches were split logs supported by pegs, and the students seated on them wore a hodge-podge of hand-me-downs. In the annual school picture, said the wags, only the schoolmarm's clothes appeared to fit.

By Addie's time some of that was changing in population centers like Kansas City and Wichita. A newly formed board of education had established some rudimentary state-wide standards. But Scott City, where Addie taught, stood on the western frontier of Kansas, out on a flat, treeless expanse, where a cyclone cellar was a requisite and the soapweeds clumped and rolled. I see her standing at the schoolhouse doorway, ringing the school bell, her black hair bobbed neatly on top of her head, her high collar prim under her dimpled chin.

There in Scott City she met the circuit rider, Preacher Carey, newly arrived from Consett, England, by way of Liverpool and New York, I assume, and an eligible bachelor. In due time, she called him Thomas. Thomas spent many of his days aiming a two-horse buggy across the tallgrass prairies and popping rattlesnakes with his whip. At the settlements he preached a fiery gospel to sodbusters and cowboys. In cabins, schoolhouses, barns if necessary, he led his services and his prayers while outside the wind moaned and maybe a windmill rattled. I imagine he was much fussed over by the women. After services they would be serving him Boston brown bread, fried chicken, egg-butter spread, boiled ham, gingersnaps. In his buggy Thomas carried home the produce that came to him as payment: turnips, cornmeal, onions, chickens, sorghum molasses, flour, oats for the horses. Thomas preached wherever he was asked to preach and covered his fair share of prairie miles, saw his fair share of prairie sunsets, and felt his fair share of prairie gusts knocking at his hat. Often he slept on the ground under his buggy.

Thomas and Addie married on November eleventh, 1901. Neither of them owned property, and where they found to live together I don't know. Probably in some vacant cabin let out by the Scott City congregation, such as it was. I can say, judging from one ancient and peeling photograph, that they washed their dishes on a school desk in front of a wood stove. They were young, far from their roots, bent on their frontier missions. Probably, for a brief time, they were happy.

Then came March 20, 1903. Who knows what Thomas was up to that Friday morning, maybe cheering an elder's wife laid up with a knife-cut infection, maybe chastising a busted-up cowboy who'd liquored his better judgment and lassoed the westbound train. Little did Thomas suspect how fate toyed with him, how the blade hung over his own hand, how the cinders were rising fast to meet his own bones. The death of Addie would lop Thomas in half, would jerk him from his saddle so hard it would put a hole through his heart. It would baffle, bruise, and bend him for the rest of his days.

Returning from his duties that Friday, Thomas must have found women scurrying in and out of the cabin and, for a time, the doorway barred to himself. Then the child arrived, entered the world, got lifted, celebrated, and clept with a long, galumphing name: George Henry Silvie Carey. I expect Thomas, in his stiff way, led a prayer of thanks. I expect he and Addie figured out what to use for a crib and just where to place it. Addie would have gathered baby clothes, odds and ends. Maybe Thomas had brought home some useful things in his buggy. But there was no good harvest to those plans. The infant screamed. Addie did not mend. Just a few days before Easter, her voice weak, her body burning with fever, she told Thomas, "Take care of George."

For Thomas it must have been an empty time, returned to that itchy frontier loneliness he thought he had escaped, fraught with guilt and looking to blame. The notion of blame repelled him, but nevertheless had crept past his mental roadblocks. The more he prayed about it and shook his head for riddance, the more blame slithered back and forth between his ears like mercury spilled on a kitchen floor, splitting itself into slippery, irretrievable droplets that rolled into cracks and crannies of his consciousness. There the poison stayed while he set about making arrangements for the colicky infant.

Because trees were so scarce in western Kansas, the soddie was a common sight on the land. The free-standing variety, distinct from the dugout soddie built into a hill, was the more comfortable in relative terms. It took about an acre of sod, cut into blocks one foot by two feet and four inches thick, to build a house with a sixteen-by-twenty-foot interior. These homes of "prairie marble" were passably warm in winter, but gloomy, the wood-frame window sometimes covered merely with greased paper. There was little ventilation, and in wet weather the roof invariably leaked. Hay strewn on the floor covered the mud to a degree, and muslin tacked to the ceiling discouraged cascades of dirt. The leather-hinged door stood low and humble; coming and going through it, a person felt the shoulders stoop, the neck crook, and the spirit sag like ticking.

On the outskirts of Scott City, an elderly German-speaking couple by the name of Kittle lived in such a place. They owned two cows and little more. For a modest fee they found space in a dark corner of their soddie for baby George. My father's earliest memory, he told me once, was of snakes crawling in and out through the sod over his crib. Thomas, for his part, always one to equate travel with solution, jumped a train to Indian Territory.

Evidently Thomas sought a salaried church position, and the Indian Territory must have held promise. At that time the Dawes Commission was at work transferring tribal communal lands to individual holdings, thereby opening the way to land sales and the legalizing of an already-present White settlement. Communities were damping down the lawless elements and setting up courthouses and churches. In this environment Thomas found a position at a church in Tishomingo, not far north of the Texas border. He settled in there to mend his emotions and make a fresh start. In 1906, sufficiently established to remarry, Thomas took as his wife a small-boned, sensitive woman, Roberta Hocket, who played the organ at the Tishomingo church. I fear this was a marriage of convenience. Roberta, a widow, had an older daughter; Thomas had George up in Kansas. On the face of things, it must have looked like a workable arrangement for them both.

George was three years old when Thomas reclaimed him, and what speech George knew was German. Thomas brought the little Teuton down to that place in Tishomingo on the Washita River. A photograph from that period shows my father as a somber child, black-haired and cleft-chinned. He looks much like Addie. He wears a Slavic-looking white tunic extending to his knees, a sagging belt around his midriff, long black socks, black shoes, and a billed hat perched on his head. His hands are clasped behind his back, making him look old and philosophical. A bleak rock-and-mortar wall rises behind him, topped with badly strung chicken wire.

George was fortunate in his stepmother, Roberta, and all his life remembered her kindness. She was quiet, accommodating, with a love of stories and song. Thomas was an altogether different sort. Though brought low by Addie's death, he had by some compensatory concatenation become, if anything, more fervent. He spouted scripture. He spouted syllogisms and doctrines of self-reliance. He was one of that type who could subvert plain reason with strict logic. He believed God spoke to him personally. Impatient and peremptory by all accounts, passionate in his pursuit of heroic character, he was not an easy man.

In Tishomingo, about the year 1910, on a spring morning after a rain, townspeople bustled on the boardwalks, exchanging greetings, jumping mud puddles as they crossed the streets.

Wagons rolled by, their wheels sucking in the mud. Suddenly an abrupt percussion rang out. The crowd knew the sound. People turned in place, staring about, awaiting some clue or word. A burly, unkempt type started down the street in an accelerating shamble. Someone shouted that Charlie B had been shot. Everyone knew Charlie B, a Black man, a turkey farmer, a harmless soul. He'd been shot through the heart at point-blank range in the doorway of the general store. The murderer kept running down the muddy street making his escape. The townspeople stood frozen. Then a small figure in a pinstriped suit disengaged from the throng. He set aside his fedora and jumped down from the boardwalk into the mud. He jumped down with the spring and lightness of a dismounting jockey. This was Thomas, standing five-foot-four inches tall in his shoes, weighing hardly more than one hundred pounds. He set out in pursuit.

The murderer fired bullets over his shoulder as he fled, but Thomas came on. The murderer turned and drew a clean bead on Thomas, but the gun misfired. Thomas closed in and attempted a flying tackle that didn't quite work, but before the murderer could shake free from the little man with the terrier grip on his ankles, the whole town was on him.

Tishomingo's city fathers accorded Thomas the laurels of a hero, but my father did not know what to do with that accolade. He had tried to write about it in those notes I found, but then crossed out his sentences with angry slashes of black ink. I managed to make out one sentence. "For the first time, and possibly for the only time in my life, I was aglow with admiration for my dad." Most surviving sons, sooner or later, by whatever means, shape their fathers into tolerable memories. My father never managed it. Those canceled sentences were about as close as he ever came.

The reasons loom clearly enough. Beatings and deprivations mounted up starkly in my father's life. In the manses, Thomas ruled with his razor strop. In the rough-and-tumble towns Thomas moved through—and he was a serial mover—there were those special trials visited upon a preacher's kid. The town of Pawhuska, for example, brimmed with all manner of frontier flimflammers and liquor merchants. They flocked to Pawhuska to exploit the newly enriched Osage people, beneficiaries of oil discoveries on their lands. Unscrupulous Whites provided Thomas with grist for the gospel mill, but their presence also pushed plenty of young toughs into the local school.

In Pawhuska, on a good day, my father might escape with a simple fistfight or rock-pelting. Those were regular occurrences. On a bad day, hounded to make public prayers as amusements for the bullies, he might have his hands bound with baling wire and get dumped head-first into a water barrel. One morning the local boys piled on him so enthusiastically, trying to force a plug of tobacco into his mouth, that his collarbone snapped. Then there was the matter of his left eye. I never understood until reading the notes how that old wound occurred—some totally unexpected local, jumping out from behind a tree with brick in hand, used it on my father's face. Afterward, with strips of his eyebrow hanging down lower than his eye, my father's main concern appears to have been the resultant beating he anticipated from Thomas.

As for the school's response to these doings, what little discipline it exerted over the students evaporated when some of the older boys tossed the principal down a three-floor stairwell, breaking multiple bones, including his back.

My father's world-view darkened in this environment. It grew, as he put it, "wormy." When my father describes in his notes certain lonely outsiders he encountered, I believe he saw in their plights something of his own isolation, something of his own role as pariah. He felt accord with the mad woman who roamed the back streets of McAlester, her neck tilted like a tipped vase. He "never forgot the look" of the Osage outcast, John Stink, who spent the last years of his life eating sardines and crackers in front of the Pawhuska general store, wrapped in his lousy blankets, mocked by children, ripe with his own stench.

Thomas laid down strict household rules—no sports, no socializing. Before and after school my father tended the family goats. "Goats" was the nickname schoolmates gave him. On weekends, and on some weekday evenings, my father attended church meetings. These were torture to him, for he never knew when Thomas might thunder out from the pulpit, denouncing some fidget, and commanding, "George, come forward!" Embarrassed parishioners would cough and look aside. My father would unbend from his pew in the back, shuffle forward, and be exampled to the congregation as a sinner, his face turning as crimson as those fires of Hell Thomas described. My father felt at those moments "deep humiliation" and "stinging anger."

Constant uprooting did not help. Every toehold my father found got pulled out from under him. From Tishomingo to McAlester, from McAlester to Pawhuska, from Pawhuska to Ada, from Ada back to Tishomingo, from Tishomingo to Winslow, from Winslow to Ardmore—Thomas kept on the move. Even his parishioners called Thomas "fiddle-footed." As my father tells it, Thomas, having had some disagreement with one church elder or another, would simply stalk into the manse and announce without warning that the family was leaving. He'd charter a boxcar from the railroad company to transport belongings and livestock. The family would be gone in two days.

On the move from Tishomingo to Winslow, Arkansas, Thomas decided that young George should ride in the boxcar with the animals. Thomas rigged pens for the chickens, the goats, and the two mules. He packed the furniture at the opposite end of the boxcar and braced it in place. Then he left my father there while he and Roberta boarded a passenger car.

My father records of that trip that the animals made odd sounds and had trouble standing upright with all the lurching and swaying going on, also that he ate his four sandwiches in two days, while the trip itself took five. He had some cooked oatmeal along, but it turned rancid in the heat. I think about my father in that boxcar with the mule and goat stale running across the floorboards, and wonder what he thought about while the wheels rolled and the engine hooted. I wonder if he milked the lurching goats.

So the isolation and the resentments build in the interstices of this notebook, between tales of this accident and that fistfight, between tales of this horse and that goat, between mentions of this or that rare friend soon lost again in another move to another town. The resentments build, push up, and jostle like water mounding against a weir.

⌒

On the Klamath River, third morning, Dev and I paddled a punishing slot. Each time we pushed out from a protecting rock, the current slammed us. Midway up, it stalled us completely. We climbed out on a ledge and balanced along it. Wind was gusting, and a blast of it caught Dev's paddle, pulling it loose. Grabbing for it, he tripped and went down like a toppled pine. Our more-or-less-constant vulnerability felt palpable and immediate. Dev held one wrist and grimaced. He soaked the wrist in the cold current, turning his hand around and around, working off the pain. He worked his fingers. Apparently everything was whole. We finished the wade, climbed into our kayaks, and paddled on.

Another problem—my kayak was breaking. An engineering megalomania had bubbled into my brain prior to the trip. I'd removed both the rear support pillar and the entire bottom of the seat, substituting an Ensolite pad. The remake allowed more room for gear and discouraged sleeping legs, but without the original support systems, the kayak's bottom rippled and bent as I paddled, bulging down under my weight. Whenever the kayak scraped rock, it made crackling sounds, like pieces of glass pulverizing under a boot. Visible cracks ran across the bottom of the hull.

Also, the unsupported rear deck was splitting at the cockpit coaming. Several times an hour I sat back on the deck to enter or exit the kayak, and the deck's consequent bending kept lengthening the split until my spray skirt no longer covered it. Whenever we met heavy waves or roil, water poured through the split into the kayak. I didn't think my kayak would last the trip, and only hoped the bottom didn't drop out in a bad place.

"I thought the gear I stuffed in there would act as a support brace."

"I guess not," Dev said, shaking his head sadly as he eyed the growing gap in the deck.

After lunch we passed by deer hides stretched on sapling frames, a tarpaper shack just visible in the bushes further back. An old yellow Plymouth came rattling down a sandy access road, kept rolling upstream along the riverbed, bouncing over boulders, keeping pace with us. For a moment it appeared the driver and his friends were trying to cut us off. No rifles showed at the windows, however; and when I saw the swimming hole up ahead, another van already parked there and skinny-dippers scurrying for their clothes, I felt embarrassed by my suspicions. The Plymouth pulled to a stop beside the van. Yet another car appeared behind us, bouncing and raising dust. Dev and I cut across to the far side of the river so as not to intrude, and paddled up behind some boulders until we were out of view.

Thunder started grumbling around the edges of the eastern horizon; darts of lightning played across the clouds. We pulled off the river thinking only to sit tight until the lightning passed. But the sky grew darker, with all the looks of a major storm. We decided to construct a lean-to, hauled our kayaks up on shore, and cast around for the best place to build. Before we had fairly started, lightning flashed almost beside us, thunder clapped so close and sharp that the ground shook, and a silver rain squalled down on us, slanted in driving sheets.

After the first panic, we looked around in wonderment. It was a warm rain. All our gear was packed in waterproof duffels, ourselves clad in swimming trunks. We were as water-proofed on land as on the river. We pushed through the deluge and hauled some fallen alder logs down the hillside to use as cross-pieces for the lean-to. The heaviest log went across the back V of tarp to anchor it down. My camp shoes, one on either end of a stick, propped up the tarp's mid-section. Dev and I managed the building of that shelter like a trained survival team, though we had never built one before and didn't know at the start what design we would use. It felt good to be so perfectly in agreement about design and sequence. The comic two-shoe prop didn't hurt our mood either.

We lay inside on our backs and listened to the rain pound the tarp and smelled the ozoned air, rivulets of rainwater running, growing, invading the tarp floor. We moved some things out of the puddles. Hunger cravings stirred us to sit up and rummage for trail mix. We each grabbed big handfuls of nuts, raisins, chocolate. There were some small gumdrops mixed in there, too.

The jogged recollection didn't focus until I remembered, in the notes, the account of supply days, when my father and Thomas would load up the buckboard in town, and after the kerosene can got filled, the grocer would slap a big gumdrop down in the spout to keep the kerosene from sloshing out during the ride back to the farm. Later, when things were put away, my father would sneak out to the shed and get the gumdrop, nibble around the top of it, and around the edges of it, avoiding as best he could the kerosene-tasting bottom.

That gumdrop reminded me of the whole family history, sweet enough on the topside, sweet enough along the high edges, but the plug-end of it fouled. Thomas made for a bitter-tasting bottom side to recollection. Whatever happened to that buggy-driving wanderer of the Kansas plains, that blushing suitor of the schoolmarm?

⇝

Some particularly harsh and brooding passages of the notes concern events in the spring of 1915, not long after my father's twelfth birthday. Hunger began it—there was never that much to eat in the household, gruel for breakfast, cornbread for lunch. School was a long walk going, and a long walk returning. My father would be hungry most of the day, every day. He'd get home hungry and be forbidden to eat. He'd look out on the back porch where an earthen crock held sausages immersed in leaf-lard.

The first sausage he pilfered made little difference, it seemed to him, the space it left hardly noticeable after he'd smoothed over the gap with a butter knife. The lifting of a second sausage, some days later, came even easier. In another week my father had about convinced himself someone must have noticed the missing sausages, and, since no one had said anything, it followed that no one must care. My father was picking up the logical constructs of Thomas, but they misled him. He ate two more sausages.

Several days later, on an afternoon of dark skies, a stern-faced Thomas stepped into the living room to front young George with this question: "George Henry, have you been stealing sausages?"

George Henry felt that question on the welts under his shirt. His body commenced to shake. "No, sir," he managed.

"Some of our sausages are gone," insisted Thomas. "We've had no guests. I didn't eat them. Your mother didn't eat them. Confess it now. You did eat them, didn't you?"

"Yes, sir," admitted George Henry.

"Why did you eat them?"

"Because I was hungry."

"Well," said Thomas. The word had the sound of a verdict. His sharp face worked. His eyes pitched from ceiling to wall. "You stole the sausages, and, on top of that, you lied to me about it!"

Thomas set off for the bathroom where the razor strop hung on a hook. It was a clear and common corridor, with a path worn in the carpet through the hallway. In an instant he returned, strop in hand. That was when Roberta stepped forward, the quiet, always-acquiescent Roberta.

She had been standing beside the kitchen doorway, listening, her eyes clouding with tears. She said, "Tom, please. Please, no. The boy has had enough whippings!"

It was something Thomas hadn't expected. He stopped still in amazement.

"He stole, and he lied."

"He was hungry!"

Thomas threw her a look that told his mind and took another step toward George. Roberta took a step, too.

She said, "Well then, Tom, if you are bound to whip someone to satisfy your sense of justice, whip me."

She didn't stand exactly steady when she said this, but she didn't back away, either. It was a challenge, the first she had ever posed him. She knew when she said it, because she knew him well, how his lips would thin down, how his jawbone would mound up lumpy under his ears as he clenched his teeth, how the anger would work itself this way and that in his face for a moment, and then sink down below the surface. She feared his cold, expressionless anger, always had, but this time something rose up into her chest and throat.

Thomas commanded, "George Henry, go into the kitchen and stay there until I tell you to come out."

George retreated, and Thomas and Roberta stood there, face-to-face, in that three-room pauper's shack of a manse. Sometimes it seems to me that my father's anger, his sudden bolts of violence, his divorce, his shadows of every sort, trace back to that instant. I think, too, that this couple, Thomas and Roberta, when they loved, loved in the dark, and that Thomas had never really seen Roberta's skin, really seen it so well, the pale freckles across her small shoulders, as when she began pulling off her blouse, defying his piety. All the while, she looked into his face, holding her quivering mouth together as best she could.

Fifteen times the strop fell, and my father, listening through the thin lathe wall, heard sharp gasps of pain and soft moanings such as he had heard before only from his own lips.

〜

Reconstructions can get shaky, but even my father sees Thomas as guiltily affected by the death of Addie. My father's features, so clearly his mother's, must have kept the wound fresh. Then there were the pious dictums Thomas lived by. As I see it, Thomas braced himself up with hammer-driven willpower. He denied his own grief, resentments, weaknesses, and tried to hold everything together with a wrapping of righteousness. I wonder if Thomas broke gradually, the way my kayak was breaking, cracks running every which way and getting longer. I wonder if sometimes he heard, deep within himself, subtle shiftings, muted tearings.

Outside the manse Thomas worked his share of charitable deeds—married people, buried people, consoled the grieving, prayed with the sick, lifted the downtrodden, fought prejudice. He didn't sell whiskey, and he didn't land-job the Osage. He always wore a top hat, maybe because it made him look taller. Excepting two brief childhood visits, I never knew my grandfather, nor ever received so much as a card from him, but I believe his essence lived on, somewhat diluted, in certain traits of my father. My mother used to say that my father was a minister to everyone but his own family. She discredited his public charm because she knew its private opposite.

There were things happening between my parents when I was young, things that circled the house like the winds of their first home in Power, Montana. What I know, I know insubstantially and cannot judge. Personal experience teaches me, however, that sons can get drawn into destructive alliances with their mothers, pitted against their fathers in a combat larger and deeper than they understand. I wonder if those same triangled forces weren't building in the household of Thomas.

I find myself casting around like that, out beyond the clear tracks of the trail, hoping for some understanding of Thomas, some hint of his direction. I try to find any positive thing I can. He has his own story, one undoubtedly refracted in my father's telling. Easy vilification doesn't stand too solidly in my surmise. I say to myself that at least his faith held solid. I recall a story my father told at a dinner gathering, a story of the time Thomas stalked a local sinner into a Pawhuska saloon. Facing jibes and threats from the saloon crowd, Thomas picked a pistol off the bar and aimed it toward the ceiling. Up in the eves a bat flitted and darted. Thomas looked around at the unshaven ranks, aimed a shaking pistol as best he could, and dropped the bat cleanly with a single shot. The bat thumped down on a table, the crowd went silent. Thomas turned on his heels, and stalked out.

My father liked the story. The B-movie hero is there. God's avenger is there. Ultimately, however, the avenger gets thwarted, the sinner escapes punishment, and the saloon doors swing closed behind the discomfited preacher. My father, as I remember, thought this story considerably more funny than edifying. He told it dryly. I should remember that tone, and not push too hard against the grain of the telling. Twisting a saloon story into a serious exemplum of my grandfather's faith makes for doubtful history. Thomas's dog-eared, much-traveled Bible might be the better evidence of faith, where it sits right now on my bookshelf, syllogisms inscribed in the margins, cryptic notes scribbled on inserted pages.

No, my palliatives sort badly, and I leave the matter there, acknowledging that one thing certainly happened in that stark hour with Roberta. I cannot help but see it. Thomas traded, finally and irrevocably, the loyalty of a wife and the remaining love of a son, traded them for the cause of a few larded sausages. From that point forward Roberta took to bouncing on her bed whenever Thomas left the manse, and as she bounced, she chanted: "He's gone, he's gone, praise God!"

The day following Roberta's flogging, my father picked Thomas's twenty-two rifle off the wall and departed from home for the first of several times. He followed the railroad tracks west. A sheriff found him a day later, exhausted and hungry, and returned him home. Thomas, again inclined to flog, got prevailed on by a neighbor to reconsider.

Five years after the flogging of Roberta, she was led from the Winslow quarters, strait-jacketed and screaming, my father helplessly witnessing once again. She was taken to a sanitarium in Texas. She died shortly thereafter. A memorabilia box I found in my father's bedroom contained the funeral bill for Roberta's body, from one Jno. L. Swank, "Funeral Director and Embalmer," Denison, Texas.

⟿

On the Klamath the storm clouds cleared off. I crawled from beneath the tarp and walked down through dripping ferns to the riverbank where my kayak sat in a newly formed puddle of mud. Rolled upright and carried to a dry place, the kayak looked better. I wiped off my feet, sat down on a boulder to stare out at the river and the clearing sky, but found myself instead looking at the delicate bones of a fish. Pain, blood, and dying had gone into that skeletal arrangement, but now the forms of it, against a wash of mud, lay finished, white, and elegant as fresco.

I did not like at all what Thomas had done with his razor strop, or what he had done another time with an oak clapboard, or what he had done another time with an axe handle, or what he had done all the other angry times, and with who knows what else in hand. I could recreate the loss of Addie in my imagination. I could posit floggings, probably sanctioned floggings, in Thomas's own childhood. I could understand, without approving it, an Old

Testament fixation on household hierarchy. Whether any of that excused anything, or mitigated anything, I could not even bring myself to decide. What I saw most clearly was how the scars worked forward, how the anger passed from generation to generation, from my grandfather to my father, and from my father on down to myself. I saw how my father's moods and flare-ups, that I had thought so immediate, held the ashes of the Territory. After I knew those stories, I could taste the ashes in all the incidents I remembered. Nothing any longer tasted small, personal, or inconsequential. Everything held that acrid flavor of legacy.

Ascendancy

We are the sons of flint and pitch.

—Dylan Thomas

Two bald eagles soared low in front of our shelter the next morning, good omens in my personal scripture. We were open to luck where we could find it; and you could say we were lucky to spend time in the maw of Kenek Canyon that day, just to have been there; but we paid a toll of bruises and fatigue for the privilege. I've heard it said that certain natives beat themselves with sticks to combat fatigue, developing attention through pain. Dev and I beat ourselves, less advertently, with ledge rock and boulder; but after ten hours of it a reverse effect set in, and we could hardly lift our legs.

The eagles disappeared up the canyon, carrying along their flappy insouciance. I crawled out of my bag and swung my shoulders. Not too sore. My legs felt looser in the hamstrings than on the previous days, always helpful in a kayak. The river looked soft and beckoning. We pulled on our damp clothes, ate some breakfast, then sharp-set the noses of our kayaks into the current. The air held scents of stone and moss. Water whished against our boats.

More and more the river changed from its earlier broad coursing to a series of pools and drops. In upstream mode, that meant pools and rises. We jumped some of the rises, gaining speed in an upstream eddy current, hitting the chute at a thin angle and riding the momentum. A forward throw of our bodies, a grab with a paddle blade for whatever rock or water was catchable, a bounce or two, a moment of strained balance, and then some side-current swirl of the upper pool would inch us over into that next level, and we'd settle our hips back down into the kayak padding with a wiggly movement that felt undulant and anadromous. We paddled and jumped our way up the river all that morning until we heard the rumble of our first major rapids and saw it ahead of us as we rounded a bend. Two Yurok men stood at the base of the drop staring at the chutes.

"Looking for salmon?" I asked as we paddled abreast of them.

They nodded. "Nothing so far," said one. "It's early yet."

They looked us over, and offered no further remark. We pulled for the first chute. A whole series of jumpable chutes mounted up gradually higher and deeper into the churn. At the final and steepest chute of the rapids, we climbed out shoulder-deep into the river, clambered past some boulders, jointly lifted each kayak up a few feet, and then were over, into a back-eddy above the drop. We were amazed, really, at the efficacy of our ascent. One of the Yuroks gave us a limp wave that we took as acknowledgment.

A headiness grew in us. Our success wasn't any stodgy father-knowledge getting passed down the line, but a genuinely mutual discovery of upstream potentials. It was one of those times when the frail human body feels itself perfectly equipped for the demands of gravity and friction. We both felt it, whatever it was—most probably some configuration of endorphins and sunshine, an in-the-groove, zonal feeling to savor, but not necessarily to trust.

Our chute-jumping had burned a lot of my energy, and I began to lose that fine edge of form. About noon, as I made a lunge up a narrow pour-off, a current pushed me sideways, drove me back against two channel rocks, the nose of the kayak catching an upstream side of one rock, the tail an upstream side of the other.

The kayak broached there, sideways, wedged against the rocks by the current, water pouring over the top deck. A hard brace kept me momentarily upright, while I recalled that a kayak in that position tends to fold up on the legs.

My spray skirt popped off the coaming. The kayak filled instantly with water and tipped over. When I pulled myself free, the current pushed me under the kayak and down the chute, an underwater wash that played out in its usual slow-motion way, the scrapes and knocks dreamlike. In a lower eddy I got my feet down to river bottom and, from there, worked my way back up to the kayak. The hull was totally submerged. River current mounded up behind it and poured over it. When I heaved, the kayak's tail slipped free and the kayak, with water behind it, blew down the chute like a couple yards of aggregate. It knocked me over backward. I caught at the tow rope as the kayak washed by and managed to swing the heavy, wallowing beast around behind a rock. Just as things looked about under control, something went *pop* in my lower back, down at the bugaboo spot of an old auto injury.

So much, I thought, for euphoria and the morning's illusion of prowess. So much for eagle-luck. Dev sailed off downstream after a runaway water bottle. I crawled out on shore, dug out my duffel, and found the aspirins. Stopping the first cramping would be important. Experience had taught me that much. I downed four tablets and dropped the aspirin bottle into my day bag for easy access. Dev returned with the water bottle. We drained my kayak, repacked it, and set off upstream again, only to hit more hard going around the next bend.

There's a Yurok tale about an upstream-traveling coyote, supposedly getting smarter as he goes, pushing back up toward the interior of things, up toward Petskuk where, as Yurok myth has it, spreads an "Inland Ocean," the source of the Klamath River. Klamath Lake, where the Klamath begins, qualifies as something of an inland ocean, so that particular bit of myth has a basis in fact.

Maybe, then, the myth of Upstream Coyote holds truth also. I feel kinship with this character because his feet get sore, his tongue gets dry, and he bumbles around a lot doing goofy things.

The story goes that Upstream Coyote, trotting along, comes upon some people eating acorns. He hangs around waiting for a handout. As a joke the people cull out some moldy acorns for him to eat. Upstream Coyote gulps these down with great relish.

"I like these," he says. "How do you make these?"

The people glance slyly at each other and tell Coyote, "Fill your boat with acorns and go downstream to Kenek where the rapids are bad. The water that splashes in will wet the acorns and make them like this."

Upstream Coyote believes this to be a fine idea. He finds a boat, loads it up with acorns, and paddles down towards Kenek Canyon. At the first rapids, the boat flips over, the acorns go bobbing off in every direction, and Coyote himself takes a lengthy underwater cruise.

All in all, Dev and I fared somewhat better in this stretch than Upstream Coyote. At least we did not lose our boats. Kenek Canyon tested us, but also gifted us with river-level insight. Consequently, I can chuckle with intimate mirth at the thought of Coyote floating down into the maw of Kenek Canyon hauling a heavy boat-load of acorns and expecting only a few splashes over the gunnels. I can laugh at this joke, but also I can feel it at the base of my spine, on my purpled shins, and in my spun and hammered sinuses.

Even now, here in the study, I can see myself at a later moment of that Kenek day, balanced above the river on a particular mist-blackened boulder, encircled by crashing drops and foaming souse-holes, and feeding Blue Water rescue rope out to a wildly bouncing kayak in midstream. This was our *pis aller* attempt to surmount a rapids that was too strong to paddle or wade and too steep-canyoned to portage. We were trying out the concept of upstream lining. My position above the river unnerved me because of the rock pile directly below, and because of the unbalancing jerks on the rope. Yet, at the very moment of my trauma, in this retrospective tableau, I now include Coyote, and find myself shaking not only with stress and exertion, but also with bursts of laughter. The pitiful song-dog tumbles somewhere under me in the current, a puzzled look fixed on his mythic muzzle, while a few thousand white acorns spin round his eyes like stars in the heavens.

Fortunately, I did not fall off that boulder. Dev, above the rapids and bent into a rope with all his might, did not slip on the underwater rock where he was braced. All the strain, twist, and tumble in those moments comes finally to a settled and frozen mental form, a kind of art. This is Kenek Canyon in the chiaroscuro of mixed luck.

I doubt we would have kept going up that whole series of heavy Kenek rapids were it not for the three days of inertia behind us and a hardheaded stubbornness in our characters, a stubbornness we increasingly admired in each other. As it was, late that afternoon, we found ourselves standing thigh-deep in a pool. Our kayaks floated placidly at heel on their leashes. Kenek Canyon dropped away below us. We were through it, and above it, but our muscles twitched like jumping beans.

Dev's face looked drawn and tight. I knew that look from my own experiences. It came from taking charge. By some unspoken agreement between us, Dev had assumed the lead. This was something new with us. Before on river ventures I had been the one to make the tough decisions and undertake the riskiest tasks. That was father stuff. I had thought it would be that way again, but it was different in Kenek Canyon, and stayed different. I was lagging, and Dev was picking up the slack. He climbed over the rocks first, figuring possibilities, while I stayed back with the kayaks. Increasingly he pulled more than his share of gear and weight over the boulders and up the chutes.

As we stood in that pool, leaning wearily on our paddles, Dev remarked, almost in a fatherly tone, that all this wading through rapids put him in mind of our early fly-fishing trips on the North

Umpqua River when we'd waded out together to some deep casting rock and I'd held his arm to keep him from washing away in the current.

"You had more weight than I did then, so you could wade better. I have more weight than you do now, so the river doesn't push me around so much."

We felt some pride at getting past that canyon, but mostly relief. Probably we should have prolonged those feelings and stopped to camp. Dev thought so. He pointed out a likely clearing not far upstream. I insisted we continue. Daylight was almost gone, but old habits of schedule kept working in me.

"I want to get to Weitchpec tonight and call Catharine. She'll be worried."

Dev just stared at me. "Look at us," he said.

"I know."

"In our shape, do you think that's a good decision?"

"We're past the worst of it," I said.

Dev wasn't pleased by my insistence. We went around this imbroglio a few times, tightly edging it the way we would edge past a keeper wave in a channel. Dev offered reluctant agreement at last, as a kind of deference, I believe.

We kept paddling, pausing often, arms dead and backs aching. We didn't talk, feeling some tension from the disagreement. A couple more slips and tumbles proved Dev's caveats justified. Finally, at twilight, with sunshine long gone from the canyon, we arrived at the confluence of the Trinity River. The Klamath and the Trinity met in a swirling eddy, almost a whirlpool, at the base of a high rock wall. In the Yurok configuration of things, this confluence marks the center of the world, the place where the Yuroks first emerged to the surface of the earth. You could just about smell the campfire smoke, if you let the imagination run, and sense the fastings and the world-renewal ceremonies this place had witnessed. Nothing overt indicated its Yurok significance. No historical marker, no concession stand. You had to know what was there. The name "Trinity River" sounded inappropriate to my ear, however. That white church steeple down at Pecwan probably had something to do with the exonym, some late-arrival types stamping their piety on the map. My mind began playing old litanies, catechisms, and creeds of Presbyterianism, memories of my churchly youth, and not ones I particularly wanted to deal with at that moment. It was hard to keep my father out of the scene, however, the way he used to thrum out the Trinity each Sunday at the end of benedictions.

Meanwhile the confluence eddy spun our kayaks. We rested and absorbed the three-sixty views and the circling ambiance. Tensions from our earlier disagreement, already faded, vanished completely as we lazed on the two rivers. The Trinity washed in from the south looking green and translucent. After its churning rush down Burnt Ranch Gorge, it came out scrubbed and elemental. The Klamath, in its channel, poured muddy, snarling froth over a four-foot drop cluttered with logs. I didn't know how its water had gotten so turbid, some mud bank giving way up by Bluff Creek, maybe, or some spalling hillside on a feeder stream. Or something else. Its turbulence held menace and anger, but the Trinity somehow tempered all that, cooled and cleared it in the circling.

Dev and I felt better for spinning there. We nodded at each other and allowed as how we each were still in one piece. At last we paddled to shore, climbed out, and waded the north side of the Klamath drop. The concrete bridge of Highway 96 spanned the river just ahead of us, and there on the south side of it, well up a hillside, we could make out a couple of roofs.

I said, "I guess that's Weitchpec."

ᷱ

The Weitchpec Store stood at the top of a long, steep path. Here and there along it I paused to pluck and eat blackberries, hoping their sugar would revive me. When finally I stumbled through the store entrance, a chunky, bronze-skinned woman stood behind the counter. I asked where she kept her phone.

"Ain't no phone."

"No phone?"

"That's what I said."

I registered my incredulity, then moped around the store, picked out two shriveled peaches, a few candy bars, and took them back to the counter.

"What about your private phone?" I asked.

"Told you before," she said, hardly glancing up from her magazine. "There ain't no phone."

"But you live here," I said.

"I live in Hoopa."

"Where's the closest phone then?"

"Hoopa," she said. "Ten miles that way. Or Orleans, ten miles the other way."

Why it mattered so much to me I don't know. There had never been an absolute commitment to phone Catharine, just one of those assurances hinged on circumstance and time. Ten miles this way, or ten miles that way, was about the average circumstance, anyhow, when you really wanted to say something to somebody, and I knew that well enough. I gave up on a phone, wandered outside, checked the bulletin board nailed to the sidewall of the building—a motorcycle for sale, a Narcotics Anonymous flyer, a newspaper photocopy about some fishing-rights dispute up at Oak Flat. Behind the filling station, a snarling, stiff-legged mongrel bounced out towards me. We glared at each other, and I walked on past him and half-skidded back down the steep slope to the river.

A rifle shot popped somewhere up by the north end of the bridge. Dev and I stared in that direction. Nothing happened, and no one came into view. I collapsed on a rock and spread out my purchases—those two old peaches, four Snickers Bars. Dev shook his head sadly and started digging through his pack for his own wallet.

"I think we need some real food."

"There's not much to choose from."

"They must have some noodles," he said. "And did you look for some tape?"

I shook my head, recalling my forgotten task to look for some tape. I felt chastened, but too numbed to worry much about my failings. Dev took off up the path. I could hear his scramblings, and a few stones rolling, as I draped my body across several outcroppings and dropped uncomfortably into sleep.

〜

In Tishomingo, when my father was seventeen and still the butt of preacher's-kid hazing, he got lured down to a livery barn one late afternoon on the pretext of watching some boxing matches. He was a sucker for anything resembling a friendly overture. Once inside the barn, he found himself surrounded by the town's young toughs. There was going to be some boxing, all right, and my father was on the main card. He could fight all of them, or one of them, his choice. They laced gloves on his hands, and pushed him into a makeshift ring. For his opponent, they led forth the town's blacksmith, a burly man in his late twenties who outweighed my father by fifty pounds.

I don't imagine the betting odds fell heavily in my father's favor. The blacksmith threw roundhouse wallops, one after the other, and stormed in recklessly. My father backpedaled, covered up, took the blows on his arms and shoulders. He had fought enough survival fights by then not to panic, and to see things coming; but his arms felt like they were being beaten with a bat. Eventually the blacksmith punched himself out, and paused, center-ring, incautiously catching his breath. At that instant my father stopped running, set his feet, and put everything he had into three fast punches to the smithy's midriff. With the last blow, his fist sank in halfway to the elbow. The air went out of the smithy, and he crumpled to his hands and knees. There he stayed, too proud to fall over, too hurt and exhausted to get up.

The hazing my father had endured for so many years came to an end exactly there, in the sudden smoky silence of the betting corner, and in the incredulous looks of the bully-boys. For several days afterward my father could hardly lift his arms, and had some trouble doing his chores in a way that escaped Thomas' notice. But the hazers had made themselves scarce.

A few months later, over in Winslow, Arkansas, Thomas took an axe-handle to my father down by the spring. My father's fists moved almost of their own accord. Thomas found himself unexpectedly on his backside with blood in his throat. This was an abrupt and brutal kind of reversal. I'm told that anxiety and guilt accompany any ascendancy of a child over a parent, and certainly this physical ascendancy was a bitter one for my father, more than he could immediately process. Before Thomas had scraped himself together and staggered back up to the cabin, my father had packed a crude duffel, patted a goodbye to the Airedales, Blizzard and Missouri, and headed out.

He didn't go far, and spent the next several months working for a sympathetic neighbor. He lived in the neighbor's barn. From the loft he could look out through the slats and across a hayfield to see Thomas doing the chores—tending goats, fetching water, digging rocks, cutting wood, splitting wood, pruning peach trees, laying fence, tending the goats some more. The work gradually wore down Thomas and his pride. He sent word to the neighbor that son George could come back if he apologized for what he had done. My father sent the reply that he would apologize when Thomas apologized.

I used to wonder why my father wore his anger so low on the hip with the hammer-thong loose, how he could preach brotherly love from the pulpit on Sunday morning and practically start a brawl in some traffic jam on Monday afternoon. I recall times he would jerk on the parking brake, bolt from the car, and brace some poor driver behind us who'd made the mistake of honking his horn. "Get out of that car and we'll settle this thing right here!" my father would shout. Car windows would start rolling up fast. Nobody wanted to fight a bone-cheeked hothead in a clerical collar.

Maybe he was so angry because he had to tend to me while my mother worked a job. He'd take me along when he went out on his afternoon calls, leave me in the car when he went into some hospital or home, and he was generally angry about something. Still, like Thomas, my father always looked the smooth gentleman. He went almost nowhere without a fedora on his head. He answered to the honorific of "Reverend." (I myself addressed letters to him in that mode until I was in my thirties.) When he wasn't threatening violence, he could be totally charming. His parishioners loved him. He was not Thomas, but a dilution of similar contradictions. He was Thomas and water.

"Oh, he's a charmer," my mother would say.

She liked to imply something hidden and dark-of-character under the charm. Certainly I saw for myself the way anger could explode in him. But I understand better now, a postmortem understanding, how his violences must have stemmed from old Pawhuska-Tishomingo survival instincts, like the muscle-instincts of a karate champion I worked with on the rivers who advised me once, with earnest concern, "Don't *ever* surprise me from behind."

My father and Thomas finally managed a reconciliation, the two pulling in their horns and edging carefully around each other. Just who apologized to whom, and in what order, the notes do not reveal, nor does it matter. They found enough accord between them to build a new cabin out of oak, each lifting their end of the crossbeams on count, then splitting and fitting their just and fair proportion of roofing shakes. They settled in before winter.

Despite the way Thomas pushed himself from dawn to dusk, his health was never robust. The demands of the new Winslow place, the feud with my father, the consequent heavy load of chores, the following house-building, the recent exodus of Roberta to that Texas institution, all took a toll that fell due that winter. An extended illness flattened Thomas out on his bunk under a pile of blankets and sucked him weak. For days his food would not stay down. His eyes hollowed, his cheeks lanked, bits of spittle held at the edges of his mouth. He mumbled prayers. He looked naked and shriveled, helpless and vulnerable. My father, alone with him up there in the Ozark hills, only the occasional neighbor stopping by, had moved from the role of adversary to the role of nurse.

It suited my father. He had always hoped to be a physician, and would have been if there'd been money for the schooling. Lingering guilt about Addie pushed him in that direction. I remember from my childhood how gently and deftly my father stitched up the family dog, Jerry, when he crawled home one night looking like someone had taken a butcher knife to his scalp. I remember another time when my father rescued a warbler from the middle of the road. He wrapped it in a handkerchief, and gave it water from an eyedropper. My father was good with his hands, gauzed my knees and elbows many times, took out slivers, lanced infections. But back there in the Ozark cabin, he'd done about everything he could think to do, and still Thomas kept wasting.

One late afternoon a bobwhite flew into the side of the cabin. It hit with a *thunk*, and dropped into the grass. My father went out, picked it up, saw that it was dead, smoothed its feathers for a moment of thought, then took it back into the cabin. He skinned out the breast of it—lean, limp, pinkish-white—and simmered the breast into a broth. Thomas drank that broth, and kept it down.

ᔕ

There at Weitchpec Dev scrambled and slid back to the river bearing two loaves of bread, some fig bars, a packet of pasta, a roll of blue duct tape, and a tube of black-rubber glue, the only kind of glue he had been able to find. He did not need to wake me. Two more rifle shots had done that already, ringing from off the bridge.

"They had some silver duct tape," Dev said, "but this blue stuff matches your kayak. It's color-coordinated."

We packed up our bags, stuffed them back into the kayaks, and set off again to find a place to camp. The river ran wide there, shallow and swift. We kept hitting gravel with our paddle blades. It was easier to walk, pulling the kayaks along behind us. We hadn't gone far, however, when I tripped and fell awkwardly sideways, slamming into my kayak on the way down. The current bumped me along downstream. Something black and raging suffused my brain. I lunged to my feet, angry at myself for being exhausted, for being slow-footed, for being old. I set off again upstream with a silent, set-jawed fury. We walked along like that. After a time, Dev came up beside me. He said, "I don't know what I did, but whatever it was, I'm sorry."

It was only the evening before, I recalled, that I had hoped to transform my habitual angers into artful fish bones. I was angry at myself, not at Dev, and told him so, but the explanation sounded flat. What caused that particular anger, where it came from, I'm not even certain. Part of it came from always being behind Dev's stiff, new, smooth-bottomed kayak. Part of it came from frustration, feeling overmatched by the river. But a part of it, too, I know, came from old corners of buried memory, old models of reaction, old sour mash of Thomas, twice diluted, an unwelcome ligature of blood and influence.

Ahead of us the water deepened and slowed. My mood lifted. We found ourselves in a beautiful twilit canyon dappled with greens and umbers. A tailwind pushed us. Long upstream eddies drew us with them. It was one of those places where the upstream mode made perfect sense.

"A reward," Dev called it.

The magic of it restored us enough to paddle and pull, lift and wobble, up two more rapids to a southern knoll with a sandbar below it covered with blazing stars—five pointed sepals, five pointed petals of yellow just folding up for darkness the way they do.

The blue tarp went down amid a few dozen baby toads. More rifle shots sounded downriver. High on the opposite riverbank, where the road leads up to Happy Camp, car lights snaked through the leaves like dry lightning. Behind the tarp I noticed circles in the sand where tall grasses had blown around their centers in the wind. It took me a minute of figuring to see how that worked, but, once I saw it, it seemed like the grasses were reaching out, enlarging themselves, balancing themselves. Those grasses were admirable models, I thought, holding at the center but keeping touch with the edges. You could get too caught up in interior matters sometimes, get sucked down into the dark places, follow the neap tide and implode. You could stumble, bang into your kayak, and go blind with inner rage. It was salutary to remember the circling, centrifugal power, the balance of grasses in the wind.

After pasta dinner, we went down and worked on my cracked kayak under the wavering cone of our flashlight. We duct-taped the hull, around and around, from front to back, until the kayak looked like a blue mummy. With river knives and Sven saw we sculpted a thick driftwood branch, padded it with chunks of foam cut from the seat, sawed careful angles. We chiseled and notched the bottom until the thing fit tight and snug under the back deck, with a slot for the seat's back edge. Wedged under the coaming, this contrivance worked as a support pillar. Over that support, the cracking top-deck aligned. We drilled the top end of the crack with a knife point, and dribbled black glue over the entire crack as thick as it would take.

That chore finished, we tossed a few toads out of the sleeping bags, swept a few dozen more toads off the tarp, measured iodine into our water bottles for morning, and lay down under a black sky. Two more rifle shots rang out from downriver. One last car ran its lights through the leaves of the north hillside. I wiggled my hips around to find some comfort in the sand, then reached up, the way I sometimes do, and rested one hand on a reassuring mass of muscle in one arm.

In the nursing home my sister and I had chosen, Clement Manor, one visiting day, my father reached over from his wheelchair and felt the muscles of my arms, first one arm, then the other. Finished with that, he pulled back the hospital gown and felt one of his own stringy, blue-veined biceps. He laughed at the difference, a sad little bark of laughter, tinged with dismay.

Four-tailed Cats

No cat has three tails
One cat has one more tail than no cat.
Therefore, one cat has four tails.

—Thomas (scribbled in his logic book)

In the clean morning light we woke to a smaller river. The
Klamath had halved in its volume, no more Trinity River
pouring into it, no more Tully Creek, Miners Creek, Moreck
Creek, Cappell Creek, Roach Creek, Mettah Creek. Below our
sandbar camp the Klamath rolled along at about the levels we
remembered from our guided trips of summers past, a far less
pushy, less insistent level than what we'd come through. All
those baby toads as well, each about the size of a gooseberry,
suggested new beginnings. They hopped around in no
particular direction, inexpressive eyes looking over the next
ripple of sand. I shook one out of my river boot at dawn, then
thought maybe I should have shaken out the first boot, already
on my left foot. When I unzipped that one, pulled it off and
shook it, sure enough, out dropped a little toad. He was
flattened considerably, and his eyes had glazed.

Despite an early rise, we loafed around camp. The aspirin-
soaked weariness of the previous day hadn't left me. My mind
felt cross-wrapped in spider web. The outer world mimicked

this mindset with leaves of the blazing stars. These stuck to my shirt sleeves when I brushed against them, serrations on the underside of the leaves embedding themselves in the cotton, a kind of natural-world Velcro. I walked back into the woods and looked at configurations of poison-oak where it wrapped in chokeholds around tree trunks and rocks, then wandered down to the river to check the kayak. The back-deck crack still wobbled under the black skin of glue; that wouldn't hold for long. But the mummy-wrap of tape should help, and it looked appropriately funky.

Dried milk over granola for breakfast, iodized water over that. Both Dev and I had been too tired the previous evening to write in our journals, so we shook the toads out of our sleeping bags one more time, lumped the bags under our shoulders, and lay there on the tarp in the warming sun jotting notes as best we could. Recalling the previous day, I readily visualized white churning water, but the individual places, the patterns of rapids, our strategies of ascent, the words we had spoken—none of these shaped clearly. I wrote about duct tape, glue, and tiny toads. The best part of that entry, now that I read it over here in the study, is the flower pressed there, the blazing star. Its yellow has faded to straw-brown, but its five petals spread themselves out long and flat like miniature paddle blades braced against the page.

Our camp of that morning lay not too far below familiar river. We would connect soon with places we knew. Already I recognized stretches of that high cross-river road. From its vantage, when I'd scouted along, I hadn't seen much heavy whitewater at all; but it's generally true that rivers and road builders work differently. Road builders, when they can, blast their way straight through a bedrock outcrop, but rivers arc out along these formations, seeking the easiest path. Consequently, rapids tend to pour in places unseen from roads, out at the tip of the horseshoe bends. Sure enough, once Dev and I got packed and on the river, we hit a heavy drop along a bedrock corner, then a second one.

Dev took routes up the middle of these while I worked the edges. Father feelings set in, and I found myself lecturing Dev on river safety. Out in mid-current he'd be hard to reach if he got into trouble. My still-cramping back contributed to the moment, my wondering what I could manage by way of rescue if it came to that. Dev was feeling particularly pleased with the way he had paddled both rapids without getting out of his kayak. My comments soured his triumph. He frowned and went quiet. I could see him working the issue around in his head trying for the right words. He said, "Sometimes, Dad, you take the joy out of things with your worry."

His words scratched up remnants of my own filial memories, my recollections of risky joys turned sour by parental judgments, and reminded me of that old irony—sons in their turns become fathers. Sons impetuously leap through fire while stuff-pot fathers hesitate, worry, direct, caution, plan, and work out their rescues before they're needed. The more one loves a child, the more this is true; but when protective love gets smothering, or dictatorial, or presumptive, fraught with because-I-said-so's and *ipse dixit* condescensions, that's not such a good thing.

There's a Yurok tale about a man who makes wings and flies about in the sky. He makes a backup pair of wings, also, and stashes them. One night, when the father is out flying, the son finds those backup wings and sets off himself into the sky. Of course, the son gets into places and situations he doesn't understand and cannot control. It's an old story—Icarus and Phaëton come to mind—sons lost in their fathers' contrivances. With our culture, it all begins when the tykes start sticking their fingers into electrical sockets. That's when new fathers get programmed to the caution. They start baby-proofing their living rooms and fencing their backyards. I remember little Dev running into the kitchen with his mouth full of blood. I remember little Dev stranded high on the side of a cliff.

Those things factor, but there comes a time when they probably shouldn't.

I said, "You're right that I worry."

Dev and I looked at each other for a moment, both wanting accord, nodded mutually and let it go. We paddled on and came to a north-side backwater adjacent to a long, steep rapids. House-sized boulders threw shade around black corners. Dev disappeared into this medieval labyrinth. I followed, pushing along narrow channels, here and there lifting over a drop. Water power had rubbed and jostled its ways through sheer stone. Boulders lay contorted and hollowed. One long archway looked like a castle corridor. Rooms opened out left and right. Boulder caves receded behind tapestries of cobweb. I pushed my way through this maze to an energized border where backwater met current. Dev waited for me there, his form silhouetted against whites of the riffling channel. We lifted the kayaks over a drop and came neatly out into sunlight on a flat pool above the rapids. All that weaving through boulders had paid a dividend in elevation.

Just below a bend Dev turned back from where he paddled ahead and made hand signals for "bear." A smallish cinnamon bear ambled along the north shoreline. It saw us and scooted into the brushy willows. We pulled over to the south bank hoping to see more of the bear, but it was gone. Since we were stopped on that shore anyway, and the warm rocks felt comfortable, we ate some gorp and crackers. From where we sat we could see the familiar take-out eddy for the Lower Klamath Trip, the overgrown path up from the shore, the dirt access road cutting down from the highway. Both Dev and I had carried a few hundred boats, a few hundred paddles, and a few hundred duffels of gear over that dirt road. It was known ground, with stories attached like signposts.

Some years back I had taken a picture of Dev at that take-out, and the print still hangs on my office wall to remind me of the moment. We'd come down one spring, just the two of us, to explore the Ikes and Bluff Creek sections, places new to us. We rode bicycle shuttle each morning, then boated down into the canyons, catching eddies above each major drop to figure ways through the potholes and stopper-waves. We were nervous and stomach-fluttery, a little intimidated by the big water and its reputation but also very challenged and happy. At take-out on the last day I took that picture. Dev's smile was wide and unrestrained, full of youthful confidence and joy, full of knowing what he could do, and having just done it.

Now we were again at that place, but across the river from it, and some years later in time, resting on stones and eating our crackers. Not much seemed to be happening there overtly, but light-warps and time-warps arced across the river. Borders crossed and criss-crossed with memory. I felt too mellowed by exertion to work out all those connections, but I liked the feeling of good memories shimmering in the current, and I liked seeing that shambling bear. Bears had never much bothered us on the Klamath, but we were always careful with the coconut-butter sunscreen that attracts them like honey.

"Who was on our guides' trip down here? After we ran it that first time?" asked Dev.

"Jennifer and Reider, you and me."

"Jon was there, remember? Remember that beef dish he cooked up in wine?"

We exchanged hungry looks, remembering beef in wine.

"Rick, too. He was along."

The riverscape prompted us. We could have pulled more of that history out of the rusty files of our recollection, if we had wanted to work hard enough at retrieval. We could have lain there in the sun listing names. But it was more pleasant to simply feel the multiple levels of connection and the crossings of time.

〜

Not many rivers could open so pleasantly to me as the Klamath, nor stretch so wide with happy recollection, certainly not that darkest river of my memory, now on the bottom side of impoundment. Back in 1959, my father heard a siren song from the northlands, and the Peace River of British Columbia became his passion.

By that time my father had long since graduated from McCormick Theological Seminary in Chicago (Class of '30), had served congregations in various towns of Montana, Minnesota, and Wisconsin, ending finally in Milwaukee. I suppose he was feeling tamed, dead-ended, in need of a defining adventure. What got him going was a television program he watched one night. A man by the name of Robert Leslie—whose book, *The Bears and I,* had garnered him some fame—took an expedition down the Peace River. The filmed broadcast of that trip intrigued my father. The whole enterprise intrigued him, but most particularly what drew his attention was the placer gold that Leslie's group found. Throughout my growing-up period our family had kicked around over a lot of western territory looking for agates, jade, petrified sponge, fire opal, garnets, any stone that would take a polish. Gold we hadn't chased, but the idea of gold took grip on my father's mind, and the Peace River looked to him like the place to find it.

The whole ridiculous enterprise returned vividly to me when I was cleaning out the Milwaukee house. A file cabinet in my father's study held yellowed folders stacked with Peace River information and planning notes. My father's initial list of necessities was brief: "Canoe yoke, K-rations, gold pans." On another sheet he had added, "Axes, rope, cooking utensils, dehydrated food, tea & coffee, tobacco, proper clothes and boots, fishing tackle, guns and ammunition, boat, sleeping bags and tent, broadax & adze, three good shovels, nails and hammers, matches & water-tight case, medicine kit, movie Kodak, grease for cooking." On yet another page he'd listed the names of ten possible partners and certain plants he could eat in an emergency: "Violet leaves, blood root, stinging nettle, cat-tails, pig-weed, lambs-quarter, Jack-in-the-pulpit, milkweed (boiled twice), fireweed, green pine-cones, shepherd's purse, dandelion, dock, ferns, ripe mayapple, mushrooms, berries."

Five maps of the Peace, Parsnip, and Finlay rivers, on a scale of three inches to one mile, fell out of a single folder. I spread them out on the study floor. Names dotting the drainages still looked familiar to me—Misinchinka, Chuyazega, Destilida, Tacheeda, Tudyah. Several letters from various branches of the British Columbia government dropped from the same file. They sported a blue crown letterhead, lending weight to their assertion that the Peace River drainage had been newly designated a mineral preserve to the contour of 2,450 feet and prospecting there was illegal. Even this news had not deterred my father. He had written subsequently to the chief of the Department of Mines, who had granted a dispensation of sorts: "No effort will be made to prevent the casual panning of the gravels."

The chief of mines had added a cautionary statement, however. "I note that you hope to pay for at least part of the expenses by panning for gold along the way, and that the idea was aroused by a TV program. I would say that the amount of gold recovered is, I suspect, a gross exaggeration and there is little chance of recovering enough gold to make significant contribution towards the cost of your proposed trip."

In his excitement, my father had begun a correspondence with Robert Leslie. Leslie's letters, also in the folder, said more or less the same thing as those from the chief of mines. "Actually one can find more dollar for dollar value dry-panning the old tailings of abandoned mines in Arizona, So. California, and Nevada than in the Peace River country—that is, unless you strike an exceptionally rich pocket as we did last summer."

But Leslie also gave exact directions to the best placer areas and creeks he and his party had found, sent detailed instructions on how to dig and pan, told us how to order canoes from the Hudson's

Bay Company, where to put in, where to take out, and added the occasional warning: "Under no circumstances let yourself drift beyond this last farm; for should you do so you would be sucked into the Canyon of the Peace, where the river, normally about a mile wide at this point, flows, or rather roars, into a canyon 60 feet wide with perpendicular walls 600 feet high, for fifteen miles of impossible waterfalls and cataracts." And on the next page of the same letter: "The Ne Parle Pas Rapids are not obvious. You won't be able to hear the Ne Parle Pas until it is too late. You must check your map with great care after the Wicked River confluence or you may get sucked into the Ne Parle Pas, and if you do, your outfit will be destroyed."

Those words elated me when I first read them as a teenager. They lighted up the dreary, curtained Milwaukee living room, put a fire in the fake fireplace, overpowered even the pervasive, reeking sweetness of my father's pipe tobacco. Soon enough, however, things sobered down.

My father had taken the family on some car-camping trips. We had canoed a few lakes in northern Minnesota. I had spent the previous summer leading canoe trips at a YMCA camp. But by any sane measure we were green for a three-month wilderness sojourn. The companion my father had chosen, some new church member named Ray, had never been in a canoe, hardly even knew what one looked like. None of us had any idea how to go about gold-panning except what Leslie's letters told us. But the plan stayed alive for a time. Maps, permits, letters, and brochures came sporadically through the mails. My father talked the church session into granting him a three-month sabbatical. For my part, I started thinking more seriously about the Canyon of the Peace and the Ne Parle Pas Rapids, feeling personally responsible for our safety.

I ponder why that was. My father was good with an axe and an adze, skillful with a fishing rod. He could build a campfire in pouring rain. But, in truth, I didn't trust his judgments, and I doubted he would listen to mine. He was more or less fearless, so far as I could ascertain, and alarmingly impulsive. In the context of the Canyon of the Peace and the Ne Parle Pas Rapids, those traits were worrysome.

One time I had watched him leap head-first off a rooftop and fall entirely through an apple tree, a dead branch clutched in his hands. That dead branch was the one he'd aimed for, and that's what he'd caught. Another time I had watched him hit the gas and bury the old Plymouth up to both axles in the loose sand of a remote riverbank. Three people had told him beforehand exactly what would happen. He did it anyhow, and it took the better part of a day to work that car back to solid ground.

Those are son-memories—not always unbiased, not always kind. But, in the first instance, I heard his ribs crack. In the second, I wielded a shovel. To my way of thinking, my father's judgments would bear watching on the Peace River.

It wasn't my own misgivings that shattered the dream, however. That happened when my father announced, "I'm not going into that country without a good rifle." My mother, benign to that point, objected. She'd seen my father and myself fight. She'd stepped between us any number of times. Also, she didn't know much about Ray. None of us did. She thought the rifle made the whole scheme a recipe for disaster. She said of my father, "He'll get mad as a hornet, the way he does, and blow somebody's head off."

There's a dam now across the Canyon of the Peace, Bennet Dam, backing up the river. The Peace backs up in my mind, as well, feels unresolved, flows nowhere, its familiarity an abstraction, its maps unreferenced by any personal event. A summer on the Peace River, if we had survived it, might have nurtured some kind of respect between my father and myself. As it was, I resented that my father had primed me to such a pitch of excitement with no outlet. I resented that he had proceeded in such impractical ways, planning his menus before he had planned his route, or before finding a reliable partner, or before figuring the costs and who would pay them. Most of all, I resented that he blamed me for the fiasco, claiming I was the one who had objected to his rifle. Probably I should have been grateful that he entertained the idea of that trip at all. His intent was genuine at the start, until the gun issue arose, and until the gold idea fizzled, and then Ray announcing he had no money. At that point, the reality of financing the entire expedition dropped into my father's lap like an anvil.

My father and I never talked much about the trip, even in the planning. I felt an odd double-edge to the idea all along, a simultaneous anger at his method and exultation at his intent. He knew what he wanted, and how he wanted it. After the trip aborted, we never talked about it again. The slaps in our slap-fights got a little harder. But we did not talk of causes. He had his excuses, I had my resentments. Between us, we had our own private Ne Parle Pas.

My father did walk me around the block once in Milwaukee, a few months after he had cancelled the trip. He said, "You and I don't get along so well. That's obvious. But maybe there's something we could do to fix that."

I said, "I don't know what."

⤺

Years later, up in Alaska, I could laugh with Catharine and the kids at the hockshop signs along the streets—"Guns, Gold, Loans." I could laugh, despite old memories, because I was up there, finally, a canoe on the roof racks, exploring the bush. Why it was that on several occasions I hit the Jeep's gas pedal and aimed the rig impetuously at some mudhole or raging creek, I cannot explain. Nor can I well explain the twelve-gauge shotgun and the box of slugs, wrapped carefully in a blanket under the baggage. I used to promise myself never to do anything the way my father did it. Now I've gone and done a lot of things his way.

On the Klamath during commercial trips we used to pan for gold when there was time to waste. Our familiarity with the Klamath extended to certain high-water side-slots, good settling places. We kept a gold pan in the maxivan and a little glass vial for the flakes. All the dredges working the river channels stirred up a lot of gold. It was easy to fossick around and find some color, pick the flakes from the pan with a tweezers, and drop them in the vial. The panning never amounted to much but entertainment, though, and eventually we lost the vial of flakes somewhere on a river road.

I like better the gold in a drop of water reflecting sun, or a campsite sandbar of blazing stars. But I admit to this—more than once I've dreamed of hidden placer loads against back-country bedrock wall.

∽

One spring, when I was down boating the Trinity River with my outfitting partner, we pulled in for breakfast at the Fish-Tail Inn.

"Prospecting?" asked a burly man at the bar. He wore a black cowboy Stetson and Mexican sandals.

"No. Not us."

He looked skeptical. "Good for you," he said finally. "It's a fool's game."

We ordered up some eggs, then listened to more of the man's talk while we waited. He talked about breakfast cereals. He talked about vitamins. He talked about kids and the people he knew who had kids. He wished he had a kid. Pretty soon he pulled up a chair at our table. He wore a thick gold chain around his neck.

"Tell you the truth," he said, lowering his voice, "this is what I'm going to do. And I'm looking for partners."

He knew where the mother lode ran in a vein through a Mexican mountain. The only problem was getting in and getting out past the *federales*. He figured we would go down there with dynamite, a giant camouflage net, and automatic rifles. We'd blow the vein out of the mountain, work it clean under cover of the net, load the gold up on a pack train of mules, then skedaddle through the jungle. If the *federales* found us, we'd keep them at bay with our rifles.

We'd rendezvous at the coast with some Cuban smuggler friends of his who'd have a boat so fast nothing could catch us.

"I've got a one hundred percent disability out of Korea," he added, pulling up his shirt to show the shrapnel scars across his side and back.

"Well," I said. "You really expect to do that?"

"Oh, I'll do it," he said. "By this time next year, I'll be a rich man."

Another fellow at the bar, blonde and brown, tobacco wad in his cheek, swung toward us on his stool. "Won't never work," he blurted, and lurched off toward the door.

It was an odd moment, one of those times when the bizarre dreams of the world fall under the umbra, when the giant camouflage net of the universe drops down across our hopes and smothers them with the patterns of what we know. I felt a pathetic brotherhood with this gold-madded stranger. He would leap like my father from the rooftop. He would plummet through the golden apples into a rib-cracked pile. I wished for him something different, something plausible, something sane. I wished for him good breakfast cereals and beautiful children.

〜

All that Peace River and Trinity River history, like that disappeared bear, still hung around the edges of my reverie as Dev and I lounged on the opposite shore from that take-out road. I recalled how the Klamath, too, had its part in gold dust history, from Weitchpec on up to Hamburg, from Hamburg on up past Horse Creek, all the way to the town of Klamath and beyond, with gravel tailings piled high along both sides of the river to show for it. I've looked at the pictured faces of those old-time settlers who chose the Klamath boondocks for home—the Attebery family, old Judge Brown, the Crumpton family, Jeremiah Lane, John Titus, Ezra Tanner, Dave Cuddihy, all those others. They came for gold, or pack-trained for the miners, or cooked for the miners, or stocked stores for the miners. I've stood in their graveyards and read the pitifully young ages of their dead. The lettering has weathered shallow and faint on the mossed-over headstones. No one much chronicled what back trails those folks followed in coming, or just why, exactly, they came, except to say, "for gold." Their motives, whatever they were, are past recalling now, and with that realization the immediate moment refocused for me. A smooth, warm stone of the beach nestled into the small of my back. The stone felt good on the muscles, and I rolled my back on it for some river-bar medicine.

We felt rested by the stop, drank some warm water, and wandered about stretching our legs. I examined my kayak. The crack in the decking had loosened from the glue but hadn't lengthened at all, a reassuring observation. The driftwood prop apparently was helping. We lifted our kayaks back into the river. The water felt pleasantly cool around our ankles. We set off again, knowing the places now, or thinking we knew them.

An upstream wind pushed us along, constantly after our paddle blades, sometimes spinning the paddles in our hands, playfully jostling and shoving. The rapids seemed like old friends, and each bend held recollections prompted by a tree, or a wave, or a cut of cliff. At four o'clock we reached Aiken Rapids, where a campground perched on the north bank. We stopped there at my urging. Dev was mellow about the stopping, though it was an earlier stop than usual. We laid out the tarp on hot sand beside the river and pegged its corners with river bags. I sat cross-legged and looked out at the high rock wall across the river. Cracks and depressions splayed across the face of it, casting intricate patterns, parquetries of stone. One lone oak jutted from a crack. I looked down at my hands. A slight tremor shook them, and the calluses on my palms looked as big and crusty as crackers. Dev had wandered off up the rocks behind me. Nothing much moved but the river, a few leaves, and more baby toads down at the water's edge. Muscles stretched in my groin. I breathed into my back and worked at the tightness. Nothing else seemed very important. Everything around me shimmered in the sun.

After a time I unbent my legs, shook a floating feeling out of my head, and climbed up to the field above the river. A yellow outhouse stood there ringed with blackberries. Beyond it lay the campground. The campground host was easy to find.

"Is there a phone anywhere around here?" I asked him.

"No phone here," he said "Maybe up at Bluff Creek Store, another mile up the road. I'm not sure."

Another mile was too far for my sore feet, and the outcome too uncertain. Heading back to the river, I followed crisscrossing paths through blackberry thickets. The berries were big and sweet. I ate some and piled some in my hat to give to Dev. Back at the tarp I found Dev with a handful of berries he'd picked for me. We ritually exchanged blackberries, laid ourselves down on our tarp, and listened to the sounds of the rapids.

I was very contented just lying there on my side, propped up on my bunched sleeping bag, listening to the river. There was no urge in me to talk, nor in Dev either, so far as I could tell, no unresolved tensions. Dev and I had everything we wanted of the moment—a day's river-memories, paddle-weary shoulders, blackberry juices on our tongues.

Maybe deep conversations would never prove so profound for us as the shared pungency of those blackberry juices. Strangers drink from the same cup, making their bond. In the hours following, they will piss the same water. Simple. One thing Dev and I didn't need, at least, was hidden placer loads in remote bedrock, that whole fool's-chase of gold, and I was glad we didn't. The only part of all that gold business we needed, really, was a river.

There were a lot of rivers out there, too, from the Washita, to the mile-wide Peace, to the Trinity and the Klamath, and maybe their sounds and seasons differed some, their lights and shades, but I'd bet they all had hop-toads along their edges come summertime, crossing and recrossing their own tracks, jumping around with those idiotic eyes blazing, looking up over the pebbles and the grass blades, full of hopes and plans and new beginnings

That was fine, I thought, so long as the vista stayed to the taut yellows of sunlight and blazing stars, no dissipating glistens mixed in, no false-plated golden dreams, no loony logic, no four-tailed cats.

Crazy Woman

What sensual eye can keep an image pure…?

—Theodore Roethke

A few last items of my father's life scatter around our Oregon place. His tax returns collect sow bugs out in the garage. Some of his books stand on our bookshelves. Slabs of polished agate from his rock collection function as coasters on the end tables. There's his tackle box in the basement, filled with tooth-raked wooden plugs. Flyers and pleas for donations get forwarded to me from charitable organizations that still have his name in their computers. These lie around on the mail table for days in an odd kind of remembrance.

If my memory of him were solid, that would be one thing; but I am aware of distortion. It was startling to discover, for example, that Robert Leslie's letters about the Peace River were dated in 1959. My recollection of that business placed it in high school years, 1956 or thereabouts. An approximate truth had settled around those events. When the real date came along, the truth of it incontestable on Leslie's letterhead, it felt extraneous and uncomfortable.

Not that it's unusual to be a little off-base in memory, or is in any way inconsistent with river images that alter with light and distance. On the Klamath, the gorbellied white of a dead fish, floating at the river's edge, turned out, when I paddled closer, to be a piece of Styrofoam flecked with algae. I lifted it on my paddle so that Dev could see the miracle of its transformation, the clarity of its dripping form, the material truth of things held up in the sun.

That same afternoon Dev mistook a distant pine root for someone fishing along the shore. Also, as it turned out, both of us misremembered the familiar canyon above Bluff Creek. What we recalled as peaceful water all the way up to the town of Orleans held only a mile or so of peaceful water and about seven miles of pushy riffles. It ought to have been a familiar stretch of river, given the many downstream trips we'd run there; but while it didn't look unfamiliar, it differed considerably from how we remembered it. Meanwhile, the water-surface wrinkled and shimmered under cats'-paw breezes. The forms of rocks and trees along the canyon walls shaped and reshaped. The look of things changed with one cloud crossing the sun. I watched shore grasses blow and remembered those circles in the sand back down by Weitchpec. Shore grasses did not really twirl, I observed, but flopped back and forth, this way and that. I could see, though, how all that irregular toss-about compassing might ultimately shape the perfect circle.

It all made me wonder what the point of a familiar river might be, with perceptions shifting and the upriver mode altering the viewpoint. I could observe the observable, but a word put to it in the morning might be the wrong word by noon. At any moment the whole structure might spawl down into the current and wash around at several levels, cleverly sorting itself out by specific gravity. There was downriver truth, and upriver truth, and neither necessarily held for long. There were sharp downstream recollections, all speed and drop and churn, and there were upstream recollections, slow and gradual, like drifting bubbles. Here and there the two truths merged, but not often enough to notably simplify the world.

⌒

One late summer in a year somewhere close to 1960, my seasonal job finished, the college term not yet begun, my father, with sudden inspiration, invited me out to the Big Horns with him for some trout fishing. We drove in rare harmony across the flats of western Minnesota. That evening we caught a South Dakota purple-clover sunset, found a cheap motel, ate juicy hamburgers along the main street, and played some pool at a local dive.

The following day, rolling into the Big Horns, we located Crazy Woman Creek, set up a camp there, and went fishing. I kept cutting the wings off my dry flies because the trout were taking nymphs. We took photographs of each other holding chunky rainbows, me in a leather flight jacket, my father in his old canvas hunting coat the color of marsh reeds, a stubble over his cheeks and chin, a busted fedora on his head, and that eternal pipe sticking out from one side of his mouth. A split-rail fence jagged along at the back of the meadow where we posed, and behind the fence rose up a backbone of high peaks.

We spent several days fishing, and ate trout with every meal. One morning, for a change of pace, we climbed a round-topped mountain. We lunched in a blue-lupined meadow beside a stream. My father, wisely, drank camp water from his bota. I myself lay down on my belly, put my face to the stream, and lapped water. Early the next morning I began vomiting. This development jeopardized the fishing trip, of course; and I expected a reprisal of some sort. Instead, my father suggested that we break camp and head back home, that we stop at the first drugstore and get something to soothe my stomach, then take a motel where I could rest up. He offered all this with care and concern and no rancor whatsoever. I was incredulous and immensely grateful. By the time we reached South Dakota the world looked promising to me again. We stopped and watched a backlot baseball game and breathed the clover-sweet air.

Anytime I want to feel good about my father I remember that trip to the Big Horns, and whenever someone mentions the Big Horns, I remember my father standing in that Crazy Woman meadow with some trout on a stick, his busted fedora on his head, and the mountains rising up behind him like solid, reliable witnesses. And whenever I think of South Dakota, I remember sitting with my father on that bench cheering the same plays, watching the same winding-up pitcher, and having our time together. That constitutes my upstream father, arrived at a new status after some struggle. He's the same father I've known all my life, but he's different. He's turned a page of himself. He has shifted like cloud, transformed like the fish-belly. He's out of his clerical collar, out of his after-shaved authority, into camaraderie, and trying to fix things.

There's a Yurok salmon-harvest prayer that Stone of Weitspus knew: "I wish many salmon would come. I want no one to have ill luck, but all to do well. I want no one to be bitten by rattlesnakes. I want no sickness to be."

That's as good a fishing prayer as any I know. It holds community, camaraderie, abundance, springtime, and mutual caring. It suggests to me why fathers and sons still go fishing. It reminds me that what grudging respect I got from my father when I was young was fishing respect, when I caught fish where he hadn't, and sometimes when it mattered, family-survival fish devoured with a high-centered-in-nowhere hunger.

Dev never developed much passion for fishing. He tried. He got good enough at tying flies to sell a few to my fishing friends. He practiced casting. He caught some fish. But he was happier looking at spiders along the shore. I kept correcting his casting. I kept wanting to fish one more hole after he was tired. He bailed out, finally, as a survival action, leaving a gap between us. He told me some years later that he liked walking into Steamboat Inn after a morning on the river and feeling like one of the guys, and he liked wading around in the cold currents, but in the final analysis of things, going fishing with me reminded him of tennis lessons.

Fortunately there were other ways to share a river. I should have guessed Dev's river bent when those silent tears started running down his cheeks up there on the main Umpqua. He was just a kid, standing there in his wet tennies on a rock slab, and I was portaging a rapids he wanted to run. He couldn't abide the portaging. As he saw it, that rapids was there to be tried. As I saw it, we were using a borrowed canoe, not mine to risk.

After that, through the years, we shared a lot of boating times, but mostly we shared them with other people—with family, with groups. So the previous winter, up on a snowy Colorado mesa, when Dev turned my way and said, "I'm free for a month this coming summer. Let's you and me take a river trip," I thought of my father in the meadows of the Crazy Woman, and I thought of my father beside me on that South Dakota ballfield bench.

Something happens post-adolescent, a role-change between parent and child, when nothing a father can do will much shape a young man differently than he has already been shaped, his nature palpable and irreversible; and the young man has not turned out so very badly after all, certainly better than the father on occasion has feared, perhaps even surprisingly well; and the father lets go of his deep-seated paranoia that something vulnerable and fundamental in himself will be subverted by the mirror-image shortcomings of his offspring, and becomes, as a consequence, different, altered, less of a martinet, and more of a gray-stubbled old fisherman with a busted fedora and a kindly heart.

⤳

Judging from what evidence I can gather, my father never managed much of a reconciliation with Thomas. I think he tried. In 1936, when he was serving a congregation in Rice Lake, Wisconsin, he decided to visit Thomas. He hopped the Rock Island line to Kansas

City, took a bus from there through Joplin, Missouri to Siloam Springs, Arkansas, where Thomas then lived. In a way so typical of my father, he told no one he was coming.

Thomas, then in his early seventies, lived with his third wife, Martha, and their young son, Tom, on a small farm just outside of town. On weekdays Thomas worked his farm and milked his dairy herd. On Sundays Thomas preached at one church or another around the area. When my father arrived at the farm, Thomas was cordial—cordial, that is, up to the time when my father took out his new pipe for a smoke. Then Thomas got that old edge to his voice.

He said, "If you must smoke that thing, George, smoke it where young Tom can't see you. It sets a bad example."

The following day being Sunday, Thomas took my father with him up to Southwest City, Missouri, where Thomas was to preach. Thomas drove the car. I can see the two of them, with their starched white collars around their necks, their fedoras perched on their heads, driving off on those rattleboard Ozark roads. Halfway there, a tire blew and the old car shuddered. Thomas pulled over, they changed the tire, and kept going, arriving late and covered with grime and dust.

Up in the pulpit, probably hoping to catch his breath, Thomas called on my father, out in the congregation, to lead the first prayer. "George, you do the praying for us now." My father was not honored. Rightly or not, he interpreted this as another test. However, by that time in his life my father had studied his Greek and his Hebrew; he knew his Testaments; he'd about memorized the *Book of Common Prayer.* He had served three congregations of his own. He was pretty good at leading in prayer. He made that prayer in Southwest City a sonorous one, replete with time-tried phrasings. He kept at it for a good deal longer than necessary.

That night my father smoked his pipe in bed. He first took the precaution of locking the bedroom door and turning out the bedroom light. When he'd finished the smoke, he hid his pipe in his shoe, ashes and all, and covered it with a sock. Just why he felt obliged to lock his door and hide his pipe in a shoe he wasn't at all sure, until he suddenly remembered a time when Thomas caught him smoking a corn-silk fag out in the barn and flogged him with a board.

My father kept a daily diary of that trip to Siloam Springs and filed it near his notes in the study. It was a sad little tome to read. It chronicled a failure. No, I don't think my father and Thomas ever did get things straight between them. You shut that boy in a boxcar for too many days, you flay his back with a razor strop too many times, you ride those iron tracks too long, from Scott City to Tishomingo, from Ardmore to Pawhuska, and you come at last to a place that's just too far, and just too deep.

⌒

Dev and I reached the long gravel bar south of Orleans in late afternoon. Willows, driftwood, and blazing stars covered the shore. Clear spots were scarce, but we found a place to camp some twenty yards back from the river. We hid our kayaks in willows, our paddles separately, and set out for town. We got some stares as we passed the first houses of Orleans and found the first public phone. Maybe it was the blue and orange duct tape wrapped around our river boots and ankles. Maybe it was the bare bruised legs, the pile jackets, and the scruffy beards.

After my call to Catharine, we hiked down to a grocery store and bought eight dollars and three cents worth of supplies. Dev allowed that the store had a little bit of everything: *Hustler* magazine, "We Love Our Troops" signs, blue-corn potato chips, and organically grown rice. I couldn't help remarking to the checkout clerk, as she eyed our attire, that we'd put in at the Pacific. Dev looked embarrassed by my swaggering and headed for the door.

One beadledom of regulation, a river-camping permit, we had failed to acquire on the ride down to our put-in. The Forest Service office in Crescent City had closed a few seconds before we pulled on the door. I had thought then, as a contingency plan, to get a permit in Orleans; but as we stood there on the street with our grocery bag in hand, wondering where the Forest Serviced office might be located, such a bow to regulation appeared more than a little nitpicky, the more so because my watch read five minutes to five. Instead, we went searching for a restaurant. The place we found had iron skillets hanging on the walls, vestiges of various settlers. We looked at the skillets and at the menus, each expecting the other to opt for steak. After polite hesitations, we discovered we both craved salad. We ordered big ones.

The back of the menu recounted bits of local history. Reading it, I learned that in 1850 a party of gold miners started up the Klamath from the Pacific in two canoes. They made it a fair ways up, somewhere close to Orleans Bar, when "their bubble bursted." I was curious what bubble bursted, and just exactly why, and maybe someone back in the kitchen knew, but the menu didn't say. What little history I do know about the place is this. Orleans Bar served as county seat from 1855 to 1875, before the county itself, Klamath County, got dissolved. County costs were exceeding revenues, mainly because gold miners, out in their riverside shanties, were a hard breed to govern, a hard breed to tax. I recalled a story about one Sammy Howard, Klamath County placer miner, reputedly neat in his camp ways. He was cooking breakfast over a bed of coals one morning when his coffeepot tipped and made a mess of things. Sammy whipped out his revolver, blew two holes in the offending pot, and announced, "No damned coffeepot is running things in this camp!"

It was almost dark when we headed back to the river. The roadsides exuded the sweetness of ripe blackberries. We turned off at a dirt path. A quarter-mile farther we left the path and beat our way across a series of dry gullies, cast around a bit, finally found our tarp glowing pale blue against the gravels of the river bar.

We were back to the solitude. A fine renegade feeling settled down on us out there on the gravel bar, willows flanking us on all sides, sounds of the invisible river washing across the cool air. We checked on our kayaks and paddles. We brushed our teeth. We wandered separate ways to find the perfect *pissoir* bush. We stumbled around, half-heartedly exploring, then found our tarp again and lay down in the gathering darkness. Orleans had been congenial enough, but we were glad to get back to the river's simplicity and to the hard comforts of the tarp over water-smoothed stones.

Swallows and bats darted and dove overhead, the swallows higher up than the bats. On a lower plane of their own, not much above our noses, hawk moths darted, as they had done previous evenings. A bright red patch on my sleeping bag hood attracted them, and they zoomed in to check it out, hovering so close that I felt the wind from their wings across my cheeks.

The patch fooled them for a flower, and then wasn't a flower, which appeared a fair fooling to me, given the shimmering and shifting ways of a lot of things, images included, memories included, relationships included. Even the darkness proved a kind of fooling when the moon rose up across the river during the night and woke me. I hitched up on one elbow for awhile watching the eerie white glow of the moonlight where it spread itself on the river bar.

Whatever shifts came and went, I thought, whatever refractions, whatever alterations of memory, we were incontestably there on the gravel bar together, Dev and myself. We hadn't shared that many words, but we'd shared a few. Also, those paddle strokes kept adding up, as did the mutual sharing of gorp and pasta. Dev's form lay there beside me, mounded and huddled, his head thrust deep into the hood of his sleeping bag. I trusted my senses enough to trust that form. I could hear his breathing. I could feel his knee against my foot.

Spans and Ruction

Oh, there is never a homewards, only a meeting,
and what you meet is what comes your way.

—Hermann Broch

Ahead of us that next morning rose up the Orleans bridge, high and curving, where the road down from Happy Camp leads into town across a northern twist of river. Before the bridge went in, a story goes, an old Karok, for a fee, crossed people over the river in a dugout canoe. A certain preacher arrived in the area and used the old Karok's ferry service some twenty times. Each time the ferryman asked for payment, the preacher tugged down the brim of his black hat and proclaimed that the Lord would be making whatever payments were due.

It happened there was a merchant in Orleans by the name of Lord. Soon enough, the ferryman showed up at Lord's store demanding payment. Lord was a generous and understanding man. He listened to the ferryman's story, nodded thoughtfully, and made good what was owing, but as he handed over the coins, he said, "Don't cross that preacher over anymore. Let him swim."

Probably no one but a preacher's kid would resonate to that story the way I do, would push past the humor and find the underside of stereotype. Preachers get detested and preachers get venerated, without much middle ground. Outside the walls of the church, a preacher commonly rates as a prig, or a scallywag, or worse, while inside the church parishioners fuss over him like a beautiful child. They wash his vestments. They clutch his hands like passports to Heaven. The polarity of views is remarkable. A preacher's kid grows up wondering if he is spawn of the devil or bloodline of Christ himself. Of course, the kid has actually seen two sides of his father—his blind rages and his beatific charms—and it all makes a peculiar kind of sense.

In the boondocks of Idaho once, myself about twelve, our family got led out to a garnet-rich creek by a crusty rock hound named Red. On the way out, Red let me ride with him in his English Ford, regaled me with Idaho adventure stories, and bestowed on me certain boon-fellow confidences. We all spent the morning digging and grubbing together in the creek-bed, pulling out the occasional big garnet with a flourish. But after the digging, when we put down the shovels to eat some sandwiches, Red asked my father what he did for a living. My father said, "Minister," and Red stood up like there was a spider in his pants. My father said, "Presbyterian," and Red said, "I'll be double god-damned."

He grabbed his shovel and pail right then and said the digging was over. I remember him standing there in his muddy boots turning his head from side to side like a cornered animal. We divided out the garnets, Red taking the best of them, and when that was finished, he slogged over to his Ford without another word, jumped in, slammed the door, and raised a considerable cloud of dust as he drove away.

Now that some years have passed, I understand Red better. I even sympathize with certain of his tendencies, which only shows how easily the gray matter veers to black-and-white thinking. So the Orleans Bridge is a good structure for me to contemplate, because it spans both edges. Its arch breaks the dichotomy of sides.

My father had his preacherly qualities, but also claimed few categorical answers and his fair share of religious doubt. He avoided messianic Bible-thumpers. He found distasteful those simple-minded arguments that ignored the variables. He didn't shine a Holy Henry smile on people, or go around promiscuously professing. The churches he served couldn't afford an assistant minister or a full-time janitor; consequently, my father did everything from selling Christmas trees in the front lot, to decorating the altar for the various seasons, to setting up chairs, to getting the programs printed and overseeing us kids as we folded them. He wrote his sermons Saturday nights and preached them Sunday mornings. He went out every weekday afternoon to make house calls and hospital calls. He comforted people, and he helped people. Like the cheap-skate apostle of Orleans, he counted his pennies; but his salary was only a pittance. He tithed, and he believed in charity. I remember my mother wandering around the house in absolute shock one morning after my father had just donated three hundred dollars in cash to a stranger at our doorstep. My mother used to check around the back yard, looking everywhere she could think to look, convinced there were codes somewhere, tramp language scratched on the fences, maps to our house. Probably there were, but written a few blocks off, down by the railroad tracks.

When I was eighteen, I learned first-hand how that panhandling worked. I'd gotten back to Milwaukee from my summer job without much spare change, and found my parents gone off on vacation to Wyoming, just where I'd come from. An interim job as a garbage collector tided me over and taught me the trading value of Hilex bleach labels. But before the first payday, I had only twenty dollars to my name, and I answered a phone call one night for "Reverend

Carey." The caller was a truck driver who said his rig had busted down.

"Please don't hang up," he said. "This is my last dime."

He had run out of his medicine, medicine he needed every day. Without it he might collapse. Already he felt terribly dizzy. He needed help quick. I told him to stay by the phone, that I'd call another local minister and get back to him. Feeling adult and responsible, pulsing with Good Samaritan sentiments, I looked through my father's phone numbers. But the calls I made didn't connect, nobody home. Finally, I called the truck driver back and told him I'd drive down myself to the hotel where he said he was stranded.

I didn't drive very fast, uncertain of the spiel I'd heard, and my fellow-feelings tenuous. On the other hand, I didn't want to be responsible for some poor guy collapsing without a dime in his pockets. When I got downtown to the hotel, an ambulance was just pulling away, lights flashing. All that night I tossed with guilt, and the next morning, as a palliative, drove out to the hospital. They were just checking the man out. I introduced myself, and promptly stuffed fifteen of my twenty dollars into his hand. He fervently thanked me. He promised to repay me as soon as he reached his home in Chicago. Later that day, feeling curious and a little stupid, I called the hospital and asked what the truck driver's diagnosis had been when he was admitted. The woman's voice rang back sweetly over the line: "Intoxication."

Iceberg lettuce and bananas were my fare for a week until my paycheck arrived and my parents got back to town. When I told my father about the truck driver from Chicago, he didn't laugh at me, or even smile. He just looked out the window for a minute.

He said, "Well, it's on his head now."

ᔕ

In the shadow of the Orleans bridge, we bent out over the decks of our kayaks to stretch our backs and hamstrings, and to dangle our hands and wrists in the cool water. We splashed our faces. What sky we could see from our vantage looked sunny with wisps of cloud to the east. A couple of juvenile crows hopped along the beach harassing their parents with importunate rasps and caws. A truck rumbled and rattled across the bridge, shaking the overhead structure. We pointed ourselves north into the current and paddled out from the shadow. Not much slowed our progress but the occasional walk up a slot, or a pause to consider a cabin with a deer-fenced garden out front full of squash blossoms. A boy standing on a northside rock and casting with a spinning rod gave us a smile and a wave. Farther upstream an old man had worked a 4x4 rig down to the east shoreline. He sat there beside it on a chunk of wood, fishing line out ahead of him in an ambery pool. We pulled up close to him, along the east shore, so as not to spook the hole, and asked what he was fishing for.

"Sturgeon," he said. "Had a big one on yesterday, but lost him. Probably a keeper."

I asked what that meant. He said, "Forty-four inches. Course if they're bigger than seventy-six inches, you got to let 'em go. Them's the brood-stock."

We wished him luck, moved past him along the shore, and Dev said, "If they could catch me, they'd have to let me go. I'm seventy-eight inches."

Just how Dev had gotten that brood-stock big from the baby I used to wrap in a sheet against my chest and haul over half the hiking trails of Connecticut, I couldn't say. Not from my genes. Not from the five-foot, four-inch genes of Thomas. But he was a big baby, nine pounds, six ounces at birth, and so slow in arriving, twenty-seven hours, that I'd smoked all the congratulatory cigars and turned mildly green before the delivery room doors swung open. He looked so oversized in the stroller, once he was into the world for awhile, that strange women would approach us, shake their heads sadly, and say, "My, isn't that too bad."

He was a happy baby with a big dumb-assed grin. He gave me the usual initiatory spraying one day when I changed his diaper. He chortled at the dog and went crazy over ice cream, just like any baby might be expected to do. Two years later, when his new baby sister, Jennifer, came home from the hospital, he wrapped his big-little hands in a strangle hold around her neck and squeezed hard. Only then did it occur to me that Dev, like his forebears, might have his complexities, and that fatherhood might have them, too.

ᔐ

In the 1936 diary of my father's trip to Siloam Springs, I found this note about his first child, my sister: "Yesterday was Roberta Ann's birthday—seven months old. I should have sent a telegram." On the next page is but a single question scrawled in big wavy letters of blue ink: "What does it mean to be a father?"

Fatherhood—it's an intimidating term, but too formal by half for the biology of the thing. As a friend of mine opined once, "When it comes to parenthood, our little squirt doesn't amount to a whole bunch." It's what comes after, matters of rearing, that keep men scratching their heads. Whether my father ever answered his question about fatherhood, I don't know. Whether Thomas even asked it, I don't know. Faced with the same question myself, I find any unqualified answer too simple. Everything about my own status as father struck me at first as fresh, unique, and pinkly baby-skinned, until the concept grew some, looked big in the stroller, and took on weight. Suddenly there was that unlooked-for sibling rivalry to defuse, which reminded me of the iron rake my sister had once imbedded in my head, and the brother-inflicted scar my sister still carries on one wrist. Fatherhood began to echo with sounds from earlier days, with screams and cries and yelps I had heard before.

I liked the teaching times, fatherhood as sharing and exchange, when the young eyes of the child widened with the father's old truth. I liked the magical times, when my watch-face caught morning light and danced it around the walls in imitation of a visiting leprechaun. That light trick was only a variation of my father's pipe-stem fairies, with acorn heads, that he playfully propped in unlikely landscapes. I liked the music times, too, strumming the guitar and singing "The Fox" in my best Burl Ives style while the kids scrambled around on all fours acting out the verses.

Those were the easy times of fatherhood. Only later, between fathers and sons, and only sometimes, comes that cabalistic, sweat-lodge passing of secrets and the medicine-bag, or a sense that it should come, or a sense in the child that it feels like tennis lessons, or a sense in the father that it is not taking rightly, or a sense in the child that the father doesn't know anything worth learning, or a sense in the father that the child shows no respect—all those dangers; but also the possibility that the child will take this knowledge and go down to the river by Kenek, as a Yurok myth has it, and lie there in the river playing dead, braving the buzzards and aided by ravens, until the Great Condor himself comes down and lifts the child up on his back into power, dignity, and adulthood.

For Dev and myself the Klamath River was a place like that, where the Great Condor had carried him high into the thermals. When Dev first surfed that big hole up at Clear Creek, he claimed that wave for his own, and in the process claimed the river for his own. Surfing a wave is a ride on the river's shoulders, anyway, on the wings of its current, a holding to the moving power that one claims, planting the flag of possession where it cannot hold in the river, but holds in the memory, and in the heart. I sat in a shore eddy and witnessed the transformation, shading my eyes against the water's power. There aren't that many times that feel so complete and meaningful, probably because things have to be just so, like a configuration of planets and stars and moons and seasons, the apices of orbit, and parabolic moments in time, to bring about that father-son distilled collision of experience, that sharing of significant first times.

I wonder if my father owned such a memory of me. Maybe some fishing moment I have forgotten. If anything, it would be that. I wish I could remember such a moment. He took me bow-hunting for deer one time, on a winter morning, though he had never shot a deer himself and had little idea of what to do. We never saw, heard, or smelled a deer, but I stood so still at the edge of that snowy cornfield, I recall, that a squirrel ran up my trousers.

I suppose my father's kind of growing up backlogged experiences he'd just as soon not pass forward. There wasn't that much he both wanted to show me and knew anything about. So we went out unblooded and unskilled together to that deer field. We went out to several trout streams and north-country lakes. We did some rockhounding. Sometimes we went to the bowling alley, to the church dartboard league, or to a rock-polishing night class over at Pulaski High. None of those experiences, as I remember them, call to my mind the Great Condor. Excepting his doctoring of my skinned knees and his filleting of pike, maybe his prowess with an axe, I believed my father to be essentially unskilled. He got no credit from me for his Hebrew, Sanskrit, Arabic, Greek, and German, nor for his understanding of the Testaments. I did feel a small thrill of pride run through me one Sunday morning, however, when a venerable white-haired bass, next to me in the choir loft, leaned close after the sermon and whispered, "That father of yours certainly can talk!"

When the all-everything athlete and particular high school rival of mine bowed his head, folded his hands, and closed his eyes in traced prayer at a high school memorial assembly my father led, I remember ignoring the prayer, studying my rival with intense curiosity, and thinking there was some mystery at work here, some tricky medicine in the air, some power that a person might control and manipulate, something beyond the obvious that I should understand and that my father understood. That was his legacy to me, I thought, tricks of the sawdust trail, all that revival-tent voodoo.

Looking back, I understand that each shared time with my father beyond the bounds of church—in a cornfield, beside a trout stream, or at a bowling alley—however fumbling and inept, was a gift, an attempt to fix things, to go further and give more, an attempt to augment the church-life legacy. But I did not see that very clearly at the time, nor appreciate it very much. Looking back, I believe that my father himself chafed some under the tight clerical collar. He joked one time that he might leave the ministry to do religious work.

His sweet baritone voice led the hymn-singing each Sunday morning. Those hymns branded themselves into my memory so deeply that now, when I tromp along some mountain path, I am apt to start humming "March On, O Soul, With Strength!" When I become aware of what I'm humming, however, I guiltily change the tune, uncertain of my feelings, uncertain of my personal translations. The legacy of hymns is closing down with me.

Of the books I found when I cleared the Milwaukee house, one was a tall purple-backed notebook labeled on the inside cover, "Secretary's Book for Hackberry Sunday School," a number of unknown names following, a half-dozen quotations from Leviticus following that, then about twenty pages scissored away and a new, steady script on the remaining pages. Above the first such page was written in my father's hand: "Snatches of writing by my mother, Addie Long Carey."

I thought at first they were poems she had written, then realized they were the lyrics of songs, some of them long and narrative: "Whistling in Heaven," "I'll Remember You in my Prayers," "The Old Elm Tree," "The Pilgrim Company," "The Blind Orphan," "Lady Elgin," "Bernardo del Caspio," "Going from the Cotton Fields," and a host of others, most of them sad, as though Addie had collected lyrics for her own early death.

> *And here fell the tears of our parting sore.*
> *Oh little did we think we should meet no more,*
> *That ere I came back from the far blue sea*
> *They would make her a grave 'neath the old elm tree.*

Whether all these songs were the fare of some Hackberry church group I don't know, but it's my best guess.

It is not such a far step from Addie's notebook to the great corpus of the western world's choral music, most all of it church music. I cling to that choral music despite myself. The masses, requiems, and glorias I have sung in various choirs always move me. When I drive alone, the tape I slip into the car-deck is apt to be Bach's *St. Matthew Passion* or *Mass in B Minor*. I suppose my musical taste is a legacy, one nurtured in the early choir lofts amid nodding basses and shrilling sopranos.

⇆

Dev and I stopped for lunch near some mossy rocks along the east bank. A sudden sting on my shin that I took at first for the work of a yellowjacket turned out to be the calling card of a water bug. A few of them had been swimming around in my kayak's slosh-water for several days. I took time to drain out my kayak and set the captives skimming off to the shoreline. Dev and I climbed up on shore ourselves, stretched our legs, ate a few crackers, and drank some water. Sated with such fare, Dev launched into song, his voice deep and resonant, his pitch endearingly imperfect.

> *My head hurts, my feet stink,*
> *And I don't love Jesus.*
> *Really is that kind of morning,*
> *Really was that kind of night.*

He flashed me an impish glance through his black beard and said, "Know that one?" I acknowledged ignorance. It wasn't the first quirkily apt lyric he'd thrown my way, either.

We paddled on and soon found ourselves part way up the Canyon of the Ikes. Once again the upstream mode made particular sense, with a strong wind behind us, long upstream eddies pulling us forward through high-rocked canyon walls, an eagle soaring overhead. We moved right along. Dev observed that he'd never looked closely at this canyon on our downstream runs, or registered its length. After running the big drops of the Ikes, he'd been too hyped up on adrenaline to notice much of anything. His remark only served to remind me that the Ikes, that upcoming series of big-water free-for-alls, was worrying me, the more particularly because the wind was picking up. It made a tight whistling sound in the confines of the canyon. It grabbed at my hat, at my paddle, at my boat, rude and unsettling. Up ahead of us I could see the runout of Super Ike, though the drop itself was still hidden by a bend of river and a protruding wall of rock. Under us the Klamath began to bounce and buck.

Lodged in my memory lay some modest claims to downriver prowess in this canyon, recollections of springtime runs in the big melt, of hanging with high braces off cliffs of mounded water, like hanging from the sky. But heading the reverse direction into the Ikes, less conditioned and less confident, grasping at what river-savvy I could muster to lessen the strain, I felt inept. An enervating worry nagged at me as we rounded the bend and began to dodge and inch our ways up through the boulder-garden of Super Ike. It was hard, uncertain going, with squirrelly hydraulics, roil and ruction, side-waves off the canyon walls. By the time we got past it, my nerves were frazzled and my arms weary. I suggested we stop at the familiar sandbar where we used to lunch on our downriver expeditions. We could hit Big Ike and Upper Ike the next morning when the wind would be down and I would feel fresher.

Dev agreed. We found the sandbar right where it was supposed to be, and set up camp. The high cliffs brought an early shade. We sat on two rocks and played a quarter-board game of go, a game

Dev was teaching me. We'd brought along a bag of painted pennies for go pieces, and a rolled piece of linoleum marked out as a board. Like chess, it was a courteous game masking military combat. While we played, another bear ambled the far shore.

The sun dropped totally away, and a chilly twilight settled across the sandbar. The dark water, pouring around a corner and flecked with foam, heaved and popped against the canyon walls. We cooked pasta and sprinkled on pepper. After dinner and dishes I sat on the tarp and watched the headlights of a car go by on the road opposite and high above. It occurred to me to climb out of the canyon. I examined the stone faces for routes and handholds, and wondered if I could make it up. I felt envy for that driver up there on the road, and an unsettling fear in my stomach. Some kind of whitewater battle fatigue worked in me. Super Ike had reminded me of how, increasingly, I found myself halfway up currents with my arms going dead and empty, my back clumping with cramp, my heart pounding and lungs gasping, no convenient eddy to catch, unable to turn without the risk of broaching in the narrow channels, so dropping backwards again, backwards over the drops, lurching for balance in my sloshing boat. Then starting over up some other route. The two Ikes ahead, linked by a long, swift canyon rush, would be more of the same. I wished I had more in my tanks to face them, more youth in my shoulders, more suppleness in my back.

Later, wrapped in my sleeping bag under a slice of stars, I played disaster scenarios over in my head. Addie had some of those sentiments, right there in her purple notebook.

> *Lost on the Lady Elgin,*
> *Sleeping to wake no more,*
> *Numbering in all three hundred*
> *Who failed to reach the shore.*

〜

When I was about Dev's age, mid-twenties, I took a teaching job at the University of Wisconsin's Eau Claire campus. It was that time of my life when I thought I knew just about everything worth knowing. My head brimmed with graduate-school hubris. I knew histories, texts, theories, methodologies. In truth, I was educated beyond my abilities. Obvious facts, like my father's "tobacco heart," had escaped me entirely.

There remained enough boyhood sense in me, however, to explore the territory. Eau Claire is situated in a beautiful part of Wisconsin, just where the white pines and the hardscrabble farms of the north meet the hardwoods and the hills stretching southwest to the Mississippi. That first year I spent my free time tromping around the sandbur hills and tracing the nettled banks of trout streams. The following summer, I invited my father up from Milwaukee to show him some of the places I'd found. There was a demand in me to share old trout-stream connection, to recreate the scenario of Crazy Woman Creek and cement the legacy of fishing fellowship.

My father came up. Just west of town ran a deceptive little stream that looked like nothing where it crossed the county road. To get to the good place, you had to hike in a couple of miles, cross over a pine-covered hill, then drop down to a meadow where the stream slowed and deepened. Rainbows and browns rose there every summer evening.

We drove out to the access bridge, parked, and ferruled the rods. My father, in that same canvas hunting jacket he always wore when fishing, his crushed fedora on his head, looked to me as he always had. Even the smells of his gear were the same, the grease on his fly line, the gunky odor of his hip boots. We set off down the path, but he kept hanging back, breathing hard. I remember a feeling of dismay, consternation, disbelief, even annoyance.

When we finally reached the meadow, my father was too tired to fish. He sat down on a stump and said he would watch me for awhile. Two big trout were rising down below us. Above us, out from a fallen log, more trout were working. Caddis flies fluttered in the willows. I was fairly jumping with anticipation. I wanted to pick my father up and push him at the river, at those trout obligingly rising as they were supposed to rise, just waiting for us. I had brought him there so we could fish together that perfect place I had found. He just shook his head at my urgings and looked at me for a moment.

"I'm getting a little older, I guess," he said, and took out his pipe.

Ishi Pishi

Pure walls of the canyon
bear the interminable kiss
of riverbed stones.

—Neruda

Thunderheads hung at all the corners of the sky, but it did not rain. We ate a quick breakfast and set off into the hurly-burly of mounding, swirling currents that pour in the canyon of the Ikes. No pointy-nosed kayak was going to block that current, or keep it back one iota; no mortal body was going to wedge its way up against it or move it one inch from where it wanted to be, the water as heavily insistent as Thomas in his brassbound rush to Zion, in his headstrong march to Beulah Land, and like Thomas broken and bent by the struggle; that was how the current came down against us, looking past the landscapes of rock and canyon, intent on the Pacific, committed to that coast, to those bird-limed headlands, to the rolling fog and the cold, flat light. We stayed close together, picking our way carefully from micro-eddy to micro-eddy, resting when we could in chop-water next to a canyon wall, one hand wedged in a crack or clutched to a protrusion. I wobbled and worried, not comforted at all by the twisted steel girders scattered underwater through this section, remnants of a bridge washed out in the '64 flood. We stepped over a piece of girder at one place where we had to wade. Its edges looked sharp and ugly.

Even the stormy sky, the stubborn water, and the girders could not diminish the landscape that opened before us, however. High, rolling hillsides sloped above the canyon, with mountain prairies scattered between the pines. An underlying change of bedrock and soil affected how things looked and what things grew. The eye recorded these changes without purely defining them, though it seemed that the scale of hill and sky had grown larger. This was the land of the Grasshopper Song, the landscape Mary Ellicott Arnold and Mabel Reed described in their 1908-1909 journal, two teachers bringing book-learning to the natives and finding one student, at least, disconcertingly apt. He showed up for four lessons, mastered four concepts (addition, subtraction, multiplication, and division), then vanished again into the riverscape, a mathematical savant gone back to the netting of eels and the spearing of salmon.

We had crossed the line into the territory of the Karok people, the changing landscape making sense of the boundary; and I tried to remember what I knew of the Ikes family, this section's namesake. There had been several prominent Karoks by that name. Men of that clan had stood all up and down this section of river on their fishing platforms. As Dev and I dragged our kayaks up a short drop, we saw a pile of fresh-cut lumber stacked on the west shore. Another fishing platform would be going up there, evidently, the old ways sporadically continuing. I wondered what those men considered when they stood so poised over the river with their spears and nets, and if they knew a salmon-harvest prayer like the one Stone of Weitspus knew.

Dev and I lifted around the big drop at Middle Ike (a guide friend of mine had gotten himself temporarily plastered under the concavity of that middle boulder) and worked on up to the base of Upper Ike, and through it, so that by noon we had passed all the Ikes. We rewarded ourselves with lunch at the confluence of the Salmon River, the "Cal-Salmon," as it is called to distinguish it from the Salmon River of Idaho. About the Cal-Salmon it is said that while the river is a Class Five, the shuttle is a Class Six. In previous years we had camped frequently at Oak Bottom, just up the Salmon a few miles, and run the tamer lower section as a warm-up to the Ikes. Few rivers hold such deep, translucent pools as the Salmon. But when it pours into the Klamath, it swirls a few times in a broad confluence eddy, then loses itself entirely in the Klamath's moil. Thirty yards downstream, the Klamath appears to be just as murky as before.

Back in the Klamath River gold-rush days, circa 1852, as many as a thousand men worked this confluence area, but only a few stayed on beyond the easy-picking times. In 1864 there was an Indian scare here, and a story endures about one Con Cane who came down from Sawyer's Bar to help with the defense. About midnight he spied two sets of legs moving through the brush and let fly with a barrage of shots. "I got two of 'em," he crowed. Morning light revealed only a bullet-riddled horse.

Dev said, "Maybe we should paddle up the Salmon for a ways."

I stared at him, wondering how seriously I should treat the comment.

He looked amused and took a big handful of gorp.

"Just a thought," he said. "I always liked the Salmon."

Actually it would have been fine to revisit that blue-green water and the deep pools, but ahead of us on the Klamath lay a major challenge, Ishi Pishi Falls. We had to get past it before sunset if we wanted to find a place to sleep. There weren't any sandbars in the approach canyon, and we both knew it.

I have heard it said a hundred times, at least, that *Ishi Pishi* means "End of the Road." Whether that's settlers' romance or Karok truth,

I'm not sure. Kroeber makes no mention of Ishi Pishi in his catalogue of California place names. But by any name, with whatever meaning, the falls makes an impressive drop, the biggest on the Klamath, a long, powerful angle of water roughed with boulders and holes. Down in Yreka once, at a Forest Service meeting for outfitters, I had watched a video of an attempted run of Ishi Pishi Falls, the only attempt I've heard about in recent history. The rafting team put on their helmets, pulled out to the lip in their big Avon, bounced off-track in the first drop, and washed into a keeper hole. The raft gyrated there for several minutes. One of the rafters took a rope and jumped off the downstream side. He tugged on the rope, with his body as a sea-anchor in the current, but the maneuver had no effect. The two men left in the raft kept jumping back and forth to the high-side tube, trying to stay upright. The Avon finally flipped. One of the rafters didn't come up for a long time. Everyone in the Forest Service room knew the story of how that rafter had gotten tangled in a rope. The shot-from-shore video got bouncy at that point, and an outfitter at the back of the Forest Service room shouted, "Shoot the damn film! There's nothing else you can do!"

That seemed right, shouting to some distant camera person, who in turn shouted to that distant rafter under the raft, who in turn had his cheeks sucked hollow, some half-born prayer torn away by water. All of that seemed right for Ishi Pishi, where the sounds of the river transform to shrieks.

Dev and I finished our lunch, took a last nostalgic look at the Cal-Salmon, and paddled on, up under another bridge and beyond, portaged a lower falls, and reached the base of Ishi Pishi at mid-afternoon. Spray floated down against our faces and over the kayaks wetting us like rain. A grinding roar filled the canyon. Chunks of foam bounced around us. We pushed up towards the base as far as we could make it, deeper and deeper into the spray, and into the chaos of sound, then pulled over to the east shore. I had hoped for a path of some kind around the falls, but there was no path, only a maze of enormous black boulders, higher than our heads, stretching out along the shore for as far as we could see. Neither Dev nor I had been down to the base of Ishi Pishi before. We always had stopped on the bluff above the canyon, at a roadside pullout there, and looked down at the distant white ribbon of the falls. Even from that vantage, the drop had always looked formidable. In those days, too, we had the luxury of climbing back into the van and driving away.

Dev and I perched on a couple of shore stones, held tightly to our bouncing kayaks, and looked at that field of boulders ahead of us. They looked endless, and they looked slippery. Our muscles were already taxed from the morning's paddle through the Ikes. I didn't see how we were going to get around that falls. Dev climbed up a boulder for a better view, and still could not see to the top of the falls. We looked up at Sugar Loaf Mountain, just to the east, and looked again at the boulders around us, and looked at each other. Dev broke through this dazed freezing of our wills.

"I'll check for a route!" he shouted, pointing inland,

He climbed up over the shore boulders and headed toward the base of Sugar Loaf Mountain, while I pulled the kayaks into the calmest spot I could find for them and twisted their ropes several times around one hand.

According to the Karoks, pains of the human body come in two colors, red and black, and are about an inch long, pointed at both ends. I felt a black one in my chest. Shifting around in the rocks where I sat didn't ease the feeling. Probably just a muscle, I told myself. Probably just a muscle was what I'd told a bill collector on a Rogue River trip some years ago, a large man with a blonde mustache who'd kept lying back in his boat and rubbing his chest. Then he'd started burping in that classic infarction routine, and things had gotten dicey.

There at the base of Ishi Pishi I checked myself over. No numbness, no burping, no nausea. Just that inch-long black thing in my chest, pointed at both ends. I rested in the rocks and took another turn of the ropes around my hand in case I dozed off.

Dev returned a half-hour later and described what he'd found. There was a pond over at the base of Sugar Loaf Mountain. We could carry over to that, and paddle across it for some progress. Into its upper end washed a now-dry overflow gully from the falls. The boulders were smaller in that gully with some gravel between them. He thought we could make it up that route.

We secured my kayak, then hauled Dev's kayak to the pond first, went back for mine, then went back again for the packs. The pond was gunky and thick with algae and weed, but I liked the smell of it—froggy and elemental, like a minnow bucket. It sat in an unlikely depression at the base of the sheer stone that formed Sugar Loaf Mountain, the center place of the Karok world.

The Karoks, like the Yuroks, had *woge* figures in their culture, but the Karoks called these transformed ancestors *ikhareyas.* Sugar Loaf Mountain was an *ikhareya.* The mountain had sons, but they were boulders. The mountain created salmon and sturgeon and kept them in a pond at its base until they were big enough to put in the river. Sweet William of Ishi Pishi told it that way to Alfred Kroeber, and all around Dev and me stood the ranks of sibling boulders, and there ahead of us lay Sweet William's sweet-smelling pond to prove the tale.

We did not bother to put our feet inside our kayaks as we paddled across the pond. We held the packs in front of us, between our legs, on the kayak decks. Frogs squeaked and dove in the algae, pollywogs wiggled around along the shoreline. When we climbed off the kayaks at the far end of the pond, water-weeds and lacy strings of frog eggs wrapped around our ankles.

The route up the wash was a tortuous scramble. It led under several splintered and sun-bleached logs, past the remnant boards of a blue dory, around more twisted bridge girders, over a few mounds of rock, up a dusty gravel trench, over another jumble of boulders, to an inlet above the falls. We made three trips. Twice, walking back, with Dev out ahead, I sat down behind boulders and massaged my chest. But finally we were done, or almost done.

Just below where we set the kayaks and propped the packs lay a series of flat rocks, and immediately beyond them the Klamath dropped over an edge into free fall. Booming spouts of frothy water erupted like geysers from below the lip. Dev thought we should put back into the river right at the flat rocks. From there, he said, we could paddle up the few remaining boils and eddy-currents to the smooth water above. I had a strong feeling that we should carry the kayaks up further, on up to the smooth water, on up beyond the twisting pattern of boils and eddies that lay in that first tilting of river.

"How can we get higher?" Dev asked, annoyed, looking at the thick tangle of blackberries and boulders along the far side of the inlet. We stood there at loggerheads. It was an old and unpleasant scenario, returned again, and I felt my stomach sink in on itself. All the closeness we had forged getting up this river seemed to drop away.

We left things undecided while Dev made the steep food-run up to the Somes Bar General Store. Before he returned, I found a way through the blackberries and over the boulders up to the smooth water. I carried my pack up and dropped it some ten feet down, off a boulder-top, onto a tiny sand shore. I didn't want to mess around above Ishi Pishi Falls, or to have Dev mess around there either. I'd seen plenty of flips in simple eddy-lines, harmless as they looked. I'd flipped a few times myself in eddy-lines. There wasn't enough energy left in me, anyway, to do much more than cross the smooth water to that far-side sandbar where we would camp, certainly not enough energy to deal with an emergency, not that there was much anyone could do, anyway, right there at the drop of Ishi Pishi.

I went over my reasoning again and again while I waited for Dev to return. Compromise or accommodation didn't feel like the right choices. Probably Dev didn't realize how close I was to my limits, but even if I were feeling fresh and strong, I would have hesitated to put in where Dev proposed. Those flat stones looked like launching pads to disaster. I looked down at those stones one more time, measuring the pitifully short distance below them to the drop, maybe fifteen feet, all of it fast water.

Dev returned down the trail and over the boulders carrying a package of Oreos and some corn chips.

"All they had," he said, disappointed.

We ate some corn-chips, and the salt tasted good. It burned on our cracked lips.

"And I brought a message for you from the storekeeper."

"What's that?"

"He's says you're absolutely crazy."

Dev held the pause, enjoying the moment.

"He's been running that store for a long time, he claims, and guiding on the river, and he's never heard of anybody doing anything like this. When I went in, he looked at my hands and beard and asked me if I was part of some expedition, so I told him what we were doing. He said I was crazy to try to paddle this river upstream. And you, being twice as old, were twice as crazy. He said to be sure to tell you that."

We laughed and felt closer for this craziness, for knowing that the paved road of acceptable behavior was way up top, way up there by the Oreo shelf and the corn-chip bin of Somes Store. We were down in the rock-bound, crazy-water freedom of the canyon. The laughter held in us, and temporarily affirmed us, but our gazes returned to the river. It would soon be dark. We listened to the booming water. We looked at the current and at the spray, and we looked at each other.

"That's what's really crazy," I said, finally, with a gesture toward the flat stones and the lip of Ishi Pishi. "And I found a way up through the blackberries while you were gone. One pack is up there already."

Dev absorbed my statements and my tone for a moment. "Okay," he said. "We'll do it your way."

I could see he was not happy about the situation. A jumble of words lay unspoken. Our accord-in-craziness, our lunch jokes at the confluence of the Salmon, all felt suddenly tangled and wrong, like that rafter must have felt caught in ropes under the flipped Avon, half-formed words rattling against his teeth. Or like those buckskin legs stiff in the morning light, felled by Con Cane, only a neighbor's horse, poor old beast, and gut-shot dead. River impressions, shifting again, evasive as always.

Dev's eyes darted left and right, the way they do when he runs something through his mind. He said, "I want to be free and joyful out here. But I'm getting weighed down with worry about this and that, and your worry doesn't help."

He gestured with his head toward the route I'd found. "How do I know I'm not going to slip on one of those boulders up there and break a leg?"

I said nothing. We picked up a kayak, one of us at each end, and pushed through the blackberries over the way I had found, over boulders, and through more blackberries, and climbed a last boulder to where we could lower the kayak down to the tiny beach. We carried up the second kayak; and, in fact, Dev did slip on a boulder and barely caught himself. But then we were down on the sand with all our gear, with smooth water there before us, and a camping place just across the river.

We crossed without problems, and pulled our kayaks up on shore. I stumbled over and gave Dev an awkward hug. I felt grateful to Dev for not testing his luck at the lip of Ishi Pishi. I felt about as tired as I had ever felt in my life, with that hollow pain deep in me, and an evil coppery taste in my mouth. We tied the kayaks off to a stunted bush and sat down in the sand. For a long time we just sat there.

"I was just counting in my mind what we did today," Dev said. "Several miles at least of Class Two, a bunch of Three's and Four's, then those two Class Six, the lower falls and Ishi Pishi."

I went over it in my own mind, remembering the rapids.

"That's about right," I said. "Ikes Ishi-Pishi Day. I think that's what I'll call it from now on. July twenty-second. Make it a holiday every year."

"Ikes Ishi-Pishi Day," he repeated. "It has a nice ring."

The sun dropped lower, and we laid out the tarp. Things felt better. That easy familiarity between us was returning. The river in front of us looked luminous and smooth. More black boulders stood above us and below us on the beach, but they no longer blocked us from our path. Ishi Pishi Falls sounded distant and faint, like a memory of itself. I sat looking out at the river, still with that coppery taste in my mouth. From across the river, way up by the road, came the raucous cry of a peacock; the hollow echo of it in the darkening canyon brought back the ghosts.

〰

I used to think the problem family lived next door, where the Polish lady screamed invective, pulled the beard of her husband in his wheelchair, and locked him out on the porch in all weather. I'd watch that drama from my second-story bedroom window and feel superior. Meanwhile, our own family hearts shriveled, unperceived by me, unacknowledged by my parents. They were in league, on my behalf, to stay together for a time. It made shells of their lives.

My mother wrote once that she had married a good and saintly man who tied her neck in seven knots. She was not happy. She read Swinburne, Swedenborg, and Kierkegaard. She played Chopin on the piano. When those activities did not cheer her, she would sit hour after hour at the kitchen window, like a *trecento* Madonna, staring at birds in the backyard. My father would be sleeping. At this point in his life, he seldom got out of bed until noon.

The summer I worked at the YMCA canoe camp, I met a prominent muckamuck of Presbyterianism, the pastor at New York's Riverside Church. When he learned my father was a Presbyterian minister, he looked up the records in his reference books and pronounced my father a leader in new-membership statistics, a pastor whose prowess at building congregations jumped impressively off the pages. This was an eye-opener for me.

I see now what my father did, how he worked his avoidance tactics. He managed his reading and studying when my mother and I were asleep. Just about the time my mother was getting up to get me off to school, he'd slip into his bedroom and crawl under the covers. In the afternoons he'd go out to do his calls. In the evenings, after dinner, he'd retreat into his study. He played solitaire in there, dealing out hand after hand, recording his wins and losses in tight little clusters of five. He filled entire notebooks with these scratches. He was good at household solitude, maybe because he'd been trained to it by Thomas; yet this was the same man who often took an hour or more after services on Sunday mornings to talk with all the parishioners as they filed past, to shake their hands, ask about their kids and grandkids, about their travels, about their health. He was never in a hurry to get home. Home was not his place anymore.

ᔐ

Thursday, August First, 1929.
Breakfast. Worked on sermon all morning. In afternoon
washed and "Simonized" the car. What a job! But it's going to
look like new. Wrote letters to John Wilson and Carl Adams.
Want Carl for "best man."
Have been tremendously happy and joyous all day. Dear
Diary, I never was so sure of love in all my life—and that's
saying something. And these next five weeks are going to go
awfully slowly. And then! I'll have a place at last that I can
call HOME.

September 5th, 1929, they were married, George and Marion, in Fulton, Illinois, at the house of my mother's parents, the David Sterenbergs. Thomas, for whatever reason, perhaps the distance, was not in attendance. The father of the bride spent the prior day in court because, in his excitement, he'd driven his car into a neighbor's cow. After the wedding the best man revved up his LaSalle and drove the bride and groom to Rockford, Illinois. From there my father and mother took their own car, Lizzie, all washed and Simonized, to their honeymoon at Lake Geneva.

Just how long love lasted, I don't know. The marriage itself lasted until a separation in 1961, with legal divorce in 1965. Thirty-odd years of marriage, or truce, or whatever. Then Ishi Pishi, end of the road.

The divorce forced my father out of the ministry. He took a position with Milwaukee County as a welfare worker in the Medical Division. He moved into an apartment on the south side and lived there with his cousin Clara, a retired nurse from Boston. In 1967 he married Mildred Vogel and lived with her in that red-brick house on the corner of 65th Street. Mildred had thick glasses that magnified her eyes. She was a merry soul and liked to laugh, but she fell over with a stroke in 1976 and did not survive it.

In 1985 my father married Amanda "Mae" Goldsmith and lived with her until her death in 1989. Mae was a chain smoker, and she coughed horribly the first time I ever met her. At the end, she couldn't walk across a room. She spent most of her time in a wheelchair. She quit smoking, finally, but my father didn't, and they argued about it. He installed a special air-filtration system in the house. I'd call him occasionally, Father's Day, or his birthday, or Christmas, and Mae would grab the phone away from him. She'd start screaming about how he wasn't taking good care of her. Catharine would talk to Mae. When my father would come back on the phone again to say goodbye, he'd sound embarrassed and exhausted.

"That's not really her," he would say. "That's just her medicine talking."

He'd tell me how tired it made him to get Mae down the stairs in her wheelchair, and into the car, and out to her doctor, and back up the stairs into the house again, how tired it made him to get out with her to a restaurant or to see friends, how tired it made him to have to do all the cooking and cleaning. He'd tell me he wasn't sleeping well, was taking a lot of Valium to sleep, but then he was drinking coffee all day long to wake up.

"Why don't you two get into one of those assisted living places?" I'd ask. "Let them help you do the cooking and the cleaning. You're eighty-six, for God's sakes. Or come on out here to Oregon. I could find you a place where they'd take care of all that for you."

"I don't know," he'd say. "I don't know. I've got a day nurse who comes by and helps a little."

⮝

I understood my father's exhaustion better that evening above Ishi Pishi Falls. Dev and I were too tired to eat. We stretched out on the tarp, and I found myself too tired to sleep, as well, one of those contradictory physical things. While Dev slept, I leaned on an elbow over my journal and roughly sketched out the dim top of Sugar Loaf Mountain where it still caught a last ray of light. A very oriental mountain, I thought, a few pines edged into the rock face and tilted out at steep angles above the river.

The stars came out and a couple of satellites skimmed across the blackness. I listened to Dev's deep breathing. I remembered a time below Middle Ike, a beach where we'd stopped once on a commercial trip, all of us resting back in the boulders under a clear sky and a hot sun. A blast of wind from nowhere had picked up the inflatable kayaks from the shore and tumbled them out into the river along with a cloud of riverbank sand. I ran and caught a last boat that hadn't sailed across the river, and paddled over picking up boats. Then I turned and saw two of the guests, without lifejackets, swimming out toward boats in the river, and the older man getting sucked downstream toward the drop below. He was trying to turn back to shore, but tiring, and getting panicky as the current pulled at him.

Out of that calm sunny sky, in a matter of seconds, all that happened. I reached the man and pulled him into my boat. He rolled on his back, legs dragging over one side. I back-paddled away from the drop and looked down at the rocks and holes and heavy currents below. The other guides and I caught all the boats, ran a rope through the bow-loops, and finished lunch. Everything had happened too fast to be real, too fast to be anything but shadow-play. We laughed and shrugged and went on with lunch thinking it all a great joke. But the older man did not laugh, and he did not shrug, and he kept looking at me strangely.

There were a lot of times when we pulled people back into their boats, or into our own boats, and did not think too much about it. In the deeper channels, if you kept the feet up, it was no great danger to be out. There were only a few times that left an after-feeling with me—that older woman caught underwater in willow roots at The Bend, for example, and that non-swimmer going down for the third time in Wildcat on the Rogue, and that overweight Chicago reporter, out to do a story. We tried to get him to walk Blossom Bar, but he refused, then went out at the top and washed into the Picket Fence, leaving me no choice but to follow him in. And then that man who went out at The Wall in Mule Creek Canyon and didn't come up again for over a minute, finally popping up right beside me where I held in the boil below Telfer's Rock. I hauled him aboard, and he didn't know who I was, or where he was, or remember how he'd gotten into the river, or anything at all about his long underwater wash down from The Wall. We put him in a raft, and he never did remember much about what had happened. But those times were the odd ones, over many seasons, and even they had turned out all right.

Mostly it was a kind of game, and you didn't worry about it. You got to feeling that rescue was easy, an inevitable consequence of the attempt. In that regard, river-guiding was bad training for the scenes of aging parents. My mother's stroke, when it happened, was not easy, and not a game, but she came through it. I'd gotten her out of a nursing home, out of her depression and panic, and into an assisted care facility that was just opening up and willing to bend on some entrance requirements. Her language gradually returned. She'd started walking with a walker.

When I left for Milwaukee, I fully expected to mount a similar rescue for my father. After all, it was just the previous day that I'd been guiding on the Rogue, pulling people to safety. I'd do the same for him. It was naive of me to be so certain, but I girded myself to do it. I would grab him somehow from those underwater branches, pull him up from the deep current, resuscitate him if necessary. Whatever it took.

Above Ishi Pishi I lay there remembering all that, shaking my head back and forth, rapping my head with my knuckles to dislodge the pain. An owl hooted behind us on the hillside. I did not want to turn this trip into a wake, to weigh down Dev's joy with my somberness, but thoughts of my father were with me. I needed to somehow push on through to a far side. I knew Dev was waiting for that, waiting the way he did each day in the upstream eddies. But the process preoccupied me, held me in a deep and somber obsession. I did not want to be unfair to Dev, but his joy was a young man's joy, filled with confidence, endurance, and eternity. Mine was not that kind anymore, and I could not change it. Sometimes that young joy surged up in me again, but then subsided, and I could not control its coming or its going.

I lay there thinking for a long time, with the stars bright and a few leaves rustling. The owl hooted every few minutes. I kept trying to hear all the notes of the hoot, especially the last one, the softer one, so I could imitate it in the morning for Dev and ask him what kind of owl he thought it might be. But when I listened hard, the hooting did not come, and when I stopped listening, the hooting would come again, and fade too quickly, fade with a breathy whisper that I could not catch, and could not hold.

Tape

If trouble don't get me,
I'll live 'til I die.

—Folk song

Four major bridges lay behind us on the river. In a day or two we would reach the fifth bridge at Dillon Creek. I had often admired the elegance of its curving swoop across the canyon. Klamath River bridges are like that—handsome, solid, with a tenor of unassailable mass. That's the impression from topside. From underneath, however, they appear darker, a little grotesque, with graffiti on the pilings and leaking water plopping down into the river from various overhead pipes. When traffic crosses overhead, creaks and groans rattle through the underbelly.

From river level, the thought is not surprising that bridges occasionally collapse, or wash out in flood. There was that bridge at Pecwan, still marked on the map. Dev and I had seen the drooping remnants of it as we'd paddled past. There was that bridge upstream of the Ikes, toppled in the flood of '64. Its corkscrewed girders had scattered down the river corridor like so much driftwood. Up by Dutch Creek, above the town of Klamath, more girders lay scattered along the riverbed from yet another fallen bridge. Judging from all that twisted steel, it would seem that bridges are deceptively tenuous items. To see that particular truth is just a matter of looking up with the right perspective, getting the time frame focused.

Tenuousness, rust, creaks and groans, leaking water lines— these things put me in mind of my parents in their late years; and my parents, in turn, put me in mind of tape. This odd gathering fits neatly in my mind—bridges, parents, tape— spinning a text of forms. My mother, for example, when in her seventies, strode around from thrift shop to thrift shop gathering woolens. She washed these, cut them, braided them, sewed them together with strong cord and with deft touch, so that the rugs she constructed would last half a century or more. Why would a craftsperson like herself, suddenly, in her eighties, begin holding her life together with the feeble stickiness of masking tape? Why would she use tape instead of glue to fix her coffee table and her chair? Why would she tape picture frames together like time bombs to fall off her walls, one by one, and shatter? Why would she tape her reading lamp where the heat would melt it? Even a cracked crisper drawer in her refrigerator wobbled with masking tape, its pieces edge-to-edge as delicately as the spring-sticks of a snare.

My father's house held the same phenomenon. This was a man who owned power saws and power drills, who kept an antique thread cabinet filled with dies, taps, and lathe tools, who prided himself on his shelves of grinders, clamps, and hand planes. He kept one entire cabinet filled with wood screws and metal screws. He owned a new sewing machine ready-to-go on its own special table. Yet, toward the end of his life, he resorted to tape.

He patched his torn trousers with tape. He wrapped his broken glasses frames with tape. The pool table in the basement wobbled like a bog-spavined horse under its wraps of tape. Tape held wads of foam to the corners of his bedstead— evidently he'd barked his shins a few times. His record cabinet had a split along one side, easily fixed with a couple of screws, but he'd covered that with tape. When I lifted the sofa to move it, one leg fell off, smothered at the dowel with dried and disintegrating tape.

I ask myself why. Were my parents too feeble, or too blurry-eyed, to do things differently at that point? Or did they simply have an altered and creaking time frame that said things did not need to last all that much longer. Did they look up at the underbelly of the crossing?

In the hospitals where my parents found themselves after their separate strokes, the taping craze continued—IV needles taped to the hand, catheter tubing taped to the thigh, gauze manacles taped to the wrist, nose-tube taped to the cheek. My parents, in their hospital beds, must have felt almost at home.

I had only to look down to the bouldered shoreline above Ishi Pishi that next morning to see my own tape job on my kayak, blue mummy-wraps holding the cracked hull together. There was blue tape around the shaft of my paddle where the two halves met. There was tape wrapped around our river shoes, holding the felts to the soles. It was all a kind of confession to the river, an acknowledgment of our attrition. We tried to retrieve what pieces of tape tore away but missed most of them, and left a trail of duct tape all up the river, tape torn from our boots, shredded from the kayak bottom, peeling from the paddle shaft. All that tape revealed the day-to-day nature of our circumstance.

Dev did his usual morning routine of stretches on the beach. I did a few less strenuous ones, and watched the play of our shadows against the rocks. We ate a breakfast of oatmeal, wrote in our journals, then taped up our river shoes one more time.

The toes of the felts had loosened gradually, pulling away, letting in sand and grit. Dev and I had spent some time in our preparations getting those felts glued on right. We had ground down the soles of our river shoes, sanded them, laid on several layers of barge cement before fitting and clamping the felts; and the felts had lasted through some hard use, but now they had begun to flap as we walked. Each morning we sat down in the sand and wrapped our shoes with tape, using first some orange tape we had, then, when that was gone, the blue duct tape from Weitchpec Store. Simple toe-wraps didn't hold, however, so we extended the wrap back around our insteps, and up around our ankles. That method held tighter, but still lasted only a day, often less. The toe section of tape would creep forward, finally pull off, and leave ribbons of tape stringing from our ankles, undulating in the current like some living thing.

So there above Ishi Pishi we taped the felts to the shoes once again. Momentarily intact, we launched and paddled up through morning mist. Two steep drops, closely linked, confronted us around the first bend. This double blockage would be what the maps called Upper Ishi Pishi. We carried around both drops, aided by a side-eddy between them. We hoped to find easier water above, water backed up by the several falls, but instead encountered two more heavy rapids. We struggled up these with shoulder-deep wades over a shifting grid of stone. At one point, just as we lifted together on Dev's kayak, an underwater boulder rolled ponderously, jostling down into a new cranny. Dev pushed back and away at the first movement of river bottom under his feet, and the boulder grazed his leg as it tumbled. It could have been calamity. Unstable boulders spooked us all up that section.

Above, beside a beach of willow-edged sand, a young couple threw sticks for three golden retrievers. The man waved at us as we paddled by; the woman peered at us curiously. The retrievers woofed at us the way dogs woof at strange objects, ran down the beach toward us, stopped and woofed again, then whined at each other with their ears cocked. The comedy helped our mood. Just then, too, the sun cleared a hill, and the air warmed almost immediately.

Around the next bend a mid-stream boulder created a languid eddy behind it, and Dev, out ahead of me, waited there practicing techniques—left side roll, right side roll, eastern style forward lean, western style back lean. When I reached the place, I simply lay out over the hull, resting in the sun. The eddy was deep green and warm to the touch. I looked down into it. Bedrock lay far below, hardly visible. I made one slow sweeping roll of the kayak, my eyes open. It felt good, a turning of viewpoint, a change of perspective on things, the eyes fuzzed with strange water, the brain, for an instant, dizzy as a spun chicken.

We ate our lunch in a rocky cove under short willows that offered one tiny patch of shade, waterbugs in both my shoes from the weedy wade to shore. They kept stinging away until I emptied them onto the ground. We pulled out our few remaining crackers to eat. The crackers had all broken. Crumbs fell out of the package onto the rocks.

"Crumbs on the rocks," I said.

"Very dry French fare," replied Dev.

I looked at the smile spread across his face and felt some solidity to the world. For me, that smile hadn't changed from the time he was two, four, six, eight. The head was bigger, the teeth orthodontically straighter, the beard blacker by the hour, but the smile looked the same to me as ever, fixed and immortal, good cheer surviving in a world of fallen bridges, fallen parents, shifting currents, grinding boulders, stinging waterbugs. Good cheer—our sauce to crumbs. We picked the crumbs off the rocks and ate them. We were long since out of cheese, dried sausage, and gorp, and badly in need of that cache up above us at Dillon Creek Bridge. We scraped remnants of peanut butter out of the jar with our river knives, then laid the blades in cracker crumbs and lifted that sticky combination to our tongues. We licked our knives clean, careful of the honed edges, tasting the steel.

A small herd of elk filed out to the river below us, dark shapes through the trees, ghostly in the shadows, not seeing us or scenting us. They drank, then faded back into the trees; and had not the smell of them hung in the air for some moments, I might have doubted them, maybe hunger visions, thirst visions. "Bull-heavy herd," noted Dev when they had gone. "Three bulls, two cows." I liked that word he used—*bull-heavy*. It had application to fathers, grandfathers, great-grandfathers—bull-heavy men of the bloodline, freighted with bollocks.

We stayed hunkered in that shade while we rested. I thought to myself how nice it would be to have a handful of salted peanuts, or a slice of smoked cheese, maybe some raisins. Dillon Creek Bridge, and the food cache there, couldn't be that much further. Surely we would reach it in a few more miles, maybe by late afternoon.

But we didn't make Dillon Creek that afternoon, or that night, or the next night either. Bats, mosquitoes, and hawk moths flitted around us in the evenings. Mallards and geese paddled in the backwaters. Lots of frogs floated in the algae mats of the slow stretches, their bubble eyes measuring our progress. The bullfrogs at night sounded as loud as jackasses, and we knew that we could always eat bullfrogs, if we could catch them.

Sweltering the next night in my sleeping bag, choosing sweat to mosquito bites, the little devils dive-bombing my exposed face like bad ideas, the hard grind of constant paddling affecting my thoughts, time feeling heavy and distant, I recalled again my father after his stroke, the pain and frustration he endured, and a line worked its way into my mind:

> … *He hates him*
> *That would upon the wrack of this tough world*
> *Stretch him out longer.*

Old King Lear and the buzzing, miserable, naked truth of things—stretched in his mind, stretched in his body, torn both places. Kent is right about it: enough is enough. I imagine that play sometimes with tape as the stage-design motif. Tape holds the backdrops together. Tape wraps around the shaky throne. The taped-together timeframe is the thing, the rusty bridge to that pitiful line: "Never, never, never, never, never." Lear's cape is taped at the torn seam; his crown is mere tape circled over itself.

Mosquitoes kept buzzing at my eyelashes while I thought about the worm-screwed torture wheel of the stomach tube and all the other paraphernalia that, for a time, kept my father alive at St. Luke's. I should have remembered *King Lear* in Milwaukee, back with that unsigned living will on the dining-room table.

⮌

On that same Milwaukee tabletop had lain my father's Park College yearbook, *The Narva*, 1926, "George 'Boots' Carey" embossed on the cover. There was George listed as president of the junior class. There he was pictured in the track-team section with his letter blanket slung over one shoulder. There he was again in the National Webster Literary Society, English literature his major. I hadn't known any of these things about my father.

His face jumped out at me from those yearbook pages, a high-contrast face—white cheeks, black eyes, heavy black eyebrows, Cupid's-bow lips over the deeply cleft chin, and a little checkered bowtie at his throat.

Why have *The Narva* out there on the table next to the unsigned living will? With junk piled everywhere, maybe it was happenstance; but then, the yearbook had been opened to pictures of classmates, two women's faces circled in ink. Maybe he was reliving old romance, maybe reconnoitering for the next wife. He'd marked the place of one such picture with his blood-pressure card— systolic 164, diastolic 72. That told him where he was, all right. I can see him sitting at that table with his college yearbook to one side and the living will to the other, the sun wheeling past his windows, the tape disintegrating around the dowels of his sofa.

At West Allis Memorial Hospital, that first morning after I arrived, the doctor who strode into my father's room was young and abrupt. In response to my questions, he said merely, "He's an old man. He's eighty-something. That's his problem." And out he walked. The nurse who'd stayed on said to me, "He's a good enough doctor. He just has no bedside manners."

St. Luke's Hospital down on Oklahoma Avenue specialized in post-stroke therapy. I decided to have my father transferred to St. Luke's. If nothing else, the location would be right—Oklahoma Avenue, full circle home again for the kid from Tishomingo on the Washita. Before the transfer, though, I sat on my father's hospital bed with the unsigned living will in my lap. Was the will something he had intended to sign? He gave back babbled answers. When I gave him pen and paper, he moved the pen around in tight squares, slipping it off the page several times, then handed me the scribble as though it settled matters.

"Can you nod your head for Yes?" I asked him.

He shook his head, no.

"Can you say No?"

He shook his head again, no, then said, "No."

"You just said it," I said.

He looked blankly back at me.

Through all of that, repeated and repeated, my best guess was that he wanted to keep trying. He didn't want to curl up in comfort and fade out. But the whole process felt bizarre, asking him like that if he wanted to live or to die, shaking that legal paper under his nose.

"How about the heroics?" I asked him. "If you have a heart attack, do you want to be revived? They might break a couple of ribs, but they could probably get your heart back to ticking."

He shook his head, no.

I asked him again, just to be sure. He went off into babble. Reluctantly, I concluded it was up to me to make these decisions. I requested a status for him of "No Code Four." If his heart started to go, that wobbly heart under the taped-on nitroglycerin pad, the staff would only make him comfortable.

During the transfer to St. Luke's my father seemed to know where he was going. He knew all the hospitals in Milwaukee

County from the visitations he had done over the years, and nodded when I mentioned St. Luke's. He sat in a wheelchair where the driver had braced it and locked it in the orange-and-white hospital van, gave me a small wiggle of his fingers as a wave, and the van pulled away. I went out to the parking lot and found my father's Buick. It seemed to drive itself back down Greenfield Avenue to 60th. The purple-brick church, the church my father served for so many years, stood on the corner where it had always stood. There were those doors we had opened and closed a thousand times. There was that bell tower I had climbed to fix the bell-rope amid a few dozen frenzied pigeons. The imitation-stone VFW Hall still stood across the street, with the Stuttgart turret rising above the lighted Schlitz sign in the window. I turned right, on down to St. Luke's.

Not any of it resembled those first deaths I remembered, peaceful and pillow-propped, those Grandma Moses deaths in gabled houses, the final farewells to grandchildren, the burials in elm-shaded family groves. At St. Luke's, in a maze of sterile hallways, my father shared a room with "Crazy Matt" who thought the room was his business office. "Turn out the lights when you go," he'd tell me, his hair sticking straight up off his head. "Be sure you lock up all the doors."

The nurses came in day after day, one after another, and removed the extra pillow from under my father's head, as though a single pillow were medical creed. He'd try holding his head up with his one good hand. I'd go down and get another pillow from a supply closet, stuff it under his head, and he'd smile and nod to me his thanks.

They took him down twice a day in a wheelchair to the rehabilitation center and lined him up in the hallway for his turn. When his turn came, therapists sat him on a mat and tried to loosen up his ancient hamstrings. He'd fall asleep on the mat, or have to go to the bathroom. He'd groan. They'd take him down to a corner and have him put plastic rings on a post. He was so exhausted he could hardly lift a hand.

It wasn't working. They had their regimen, and he hadn't the strength for it, partly because he couldn't eat. The paralysis affected his swallowing. He kept choking on his food, inhaling fluids into his lungs. He came down with pneumonia and got transferred up to the fourth floor for recovery.

The doctors started talking to me in the hallways. They had already inserted a nose tube, trying to get some food down my father. They wanted something more permanent, a stomach tube. Another doctor took me aside and told me pneumonia was a great friend of the old.

I had been "talking" with my father about heroic measures, checking what he wanted done, still hoping for some guidance. I understood him, again, to want to keep going as long as he could, but not to want heroics. "Heroics" proved a shifty word, however. The pneumonia advocate believed that a stomach tube was a heroic measure. The rehabilitation advocates believed otherwise. The program director called me into a staff meeting where various therapists testified to my father's progress. They said to me, "Try the stomach tube. Starvation is a horrible death."

The program director gave me ten minutes to make the decisions. Do we keep giving the intravenous antibiotic? Do we put in the stomach tube? Or do we not? I walked up and down the hallways. I went outside and found a parking ticket on the Buick. I went back inside where the pneumonia advocate found me. He said starvation was not such a bad death; pneumonia would probably do the job before starvation, anyway. Then a nurse found me and advised for the stomach tube. My head spun with it all.

I sat down in the lobby beside a potted jungle plant and recalled a time in high school when I had broken up with a girlfriend, gone heartsick, and wouldn't eat. My father watched that go on for a few days. One evening he got up from the dinner table, led me out onto the porch, and stood me there. He looked me up and down. He might have smiled. He said, "Don't think you're the only one who ever felt that way. Now go in there and eat your dinner."

I found the program director in her office. "Keep up the antibiotics," I told her. "Put in the stomach tube."

By then it was late. I drove back to the house, eased the Buick into the garage, went into the house through the back door, smelled the reek of pipe tobacco, saw more tape wrapped around a broken chair rung, went into the bedroom, and lay down on my father's bed. I looked up at the walls the way he had looked up at them, looked out the back window at the streetlight of 64th, looked over at the photograph of Mount Moran, up there on his wall. My father loved the Tetons. He loved the straight-up, point-in-time solidity of that range.

⤳

The next day Dev and I passed the first gold dredge we had seen on the trip. It had gouged unnatural channels all down the riverbed, making the currents hard to read. The pools circled the wrong ways in the wrong places, eddies running sideways or backwards, shorelines weirdly deep, and mid-river shallowed with sludge. Dredging made the river arbitrary. My cheese-deprived brain reeled at the artifice. If you scooped out the rivers and skewed the currents, then all related patterns of the world guttered and warped. That was what I believed, and I did not like people grubbing with this medicine river, this natural and ordered place where Dev and I could paddle easily beside each other, and where my family history was just starting to make some sense. I did not like how side-currents came from where they should not reasonably have come, and how they pushed me against the pontoons of the dredge as I tried to get past it.

There were going to be a lot more dredges further on upstream, too. I knew that for a fact, remembering all the places where I had seen dredges in years past, remembering the Forty-niners Club and those pay-to-pan claims they owned between Happy Camp and Seied Valley.

Dev and I agreed without hesitation on our camp for that evening—an open, sandy, east-facing spit with a big eddy out front. It was five o'clock and still hot when we stopped paddling. We sat in the eddy for a minute when we reached it, catching our breath, then did a couple of rolls to informally shower. Even that submersion didn't refresh me much. We'd come a long ways up the Klamath. I'd expected to paddle myself back into shape, to connect somewhere with a downstream version of myself. I harbored a hope that the body would pull off another of its miracles, harden to the work, turn stronger for all the pain and trouble. In the past it had done that, amazing me the way it adapted to strain, to long stretches without sleep. For the moment, however, that wasn't working. I felt drained by the constant paddling. It pleased me to stop early on this wide beach. I pulled my kayak up onto the bank, flipped it over, examined its woeful bottom, and cut off long streamers of peeling tape.

The kayak's bottom looked about the way I felt. I lay back into the hot sand and took slow, deep breaths of the furnace air. I looked up far and deep into the shimmering sky. At least I was still on a river, not in some sterile ward. And maybe tomorrow we would reach Dillon Creek Bridge, and the cache there with its cheese and its raisins.

After a time, I sat up again, pulled my river-knife from its sheath, and cut wraps of tape from around my ankles. I cut more wraps from around my insteps. Tomorrow I would tape the shoes again, tape the insteps, tape the ankles, but for this day I was finished. I tugged the torn and flapping river shoes off my feet and tossed them into the sand.

Caches

A love harder to chew than an iron bar.

—Francois Villon

It was early evening and intensely hot when we paddled around a bend and saw ahead of us the distant sweep of Dillon Creek Bridge. Some teenage boys swimming in a big eddy of the bend chased out into the current to tip us over, their juvenile glands intent on mayhem. We easily paddled around them, avoiding their reach. A teepee stood under some alders just back from the shore. A man sitting cross-legged on the beach shrugged his shoulders at us and shouted, "They're not my kids!" We nodded, laughed, and paddled on, relieved to see the bridge, and to know our cache was near.

We pulled to shore under the bridge, and felt momentarily cooled by the shadow of its arch. The climb from below the bridge up to the road was brushy and brambly, but hunger motivated us. We'd come more than far enough on Oreos and corn chips. Our marker, a broken branch beside a bulldozer track, lay where we'd left it; but we weren't certain our cache would still be where we had buried it. One never can be certain with caches, and ours was no sturdy, axe-hewn, Yukon-style structure out of north-country trapper times. Our cache lay buried under a pile of dirt, rock, and half-burned slash at the end of a mining-claim double-track into scrub oak. The cache didn't hold pemmican, flour, salt, sugar, and tea, either, but only a few cans of sardines and kippers, some peanuts and peanut butter, crackers, pasta, and a bag of gorp. Dev had triple-bagged these supplies in black trash bags to keep in the scents and tied a note on the package that read: "This is a food cache. To be picked up about July 25. Please do not disturb."

We had buried it, covered it with stones, logs, and brush, then swept out our tracks with a branch of manzanita, like a couple of hoot owls stashing booty.

That had been only two weeks back, but as we climbed up from the river, it seemed like a long time ago. We had worried that maybe a bear would sniff it out, or that maybe the owner of that claim would slice up our cache with his dozer blade. But when we got to the place again, the mound looked undisturbed. We rolled off the rocks and scratched away the dirt. It was all there, not even a hole in the plastic. Everything remained just as we'd left it, even the note still clean and legible.

"We hit it exact," I said. "The twenty-fifth."

Dev broke out laughing as I hoisted the black sack over one shoulder. He said, "You look like a pirate with that bandanna on your head and that knife in your vest."

The day had been long, hot, frustrating, and Dev's laughter sounded good, because earlier in the day, after tripping a few times on the flopping felts of my river boots, and getting my kayak stuck on rocks, tripping again, and then flipping over trying to get out of the kayak below a rapids, on and on, hour after hour, I'd finally thrown a curse at the river and gone black-silent. Dev had paddled up cautiously beside me and said, "It seems to me you set pretty high standards for yourself."

Perfectionism—not a particularly happy tradition. It buoys the world view that to err is awful, that to fall short is to fail. It's one of those autogenic gods we use to terrorize ourselves. I confess I pay obeisance to it more often than not, and that tendency, I'm afraid, puts me in league with Thomas. A notebook of his that my father saved bulges with maxims of the ilk. "Finish everything you undertake, for the mental discipline of success." "Men with energy of character bend circumstances to their own purposes and ends." "No people can be highly civilized amongst whom delectation takes the place of duty." "Whatsoever thy hand findeth to do, do it with thy might!" "Work hard for ten years, and then you can work harder." Etcetera, etcetera.

Mid-afternoon we'd run into a group of kayakers from the Otter Bar Kayaking School, busy with water fights and assorted games. They had looked us over, not saying anything, until one of them, apparently the leader, paddled over and asked, "What are you guys doing—working your way upstream?"

"*Working* is right." I replied, mopping some sweat out of my eyes.

Being a kayaker, and a good one, he knew what we had faced. He kept shaking his head.

"Where'd you put in?"

"At the mouth."

He digested that. "I'll be damned," he said finally.

The two modes—downstream and upstream—floated there together while we palavered, the differences apparent—laughter and play in one corner, sweat and strain in the other. Downstream made its sense, until you'd sated of play, fed full for the moment. On our own commercial trips we'd even carried a floating Frisbee that got tossed around. We'd done the Virginia Reel in our boats, requiring just a touch of upstream work in leading to the head of the line. There had been good talk, and plenty of laughter, all spaced by the sobering drops. Dev and I remembered all that while we watched the Otter Bar group float past and disappear around a bend. We remembered all that play, all that "delectation," and valued it, but had other things in mind. We turned back from our watching, back into the current, back to our upstream work.

So Dev's laughter at my piratical looks came as a good close to a hard day. We had earned some miles, and we had found our food. The cache felt like a magical bundle when we plucked it out of the ground, and it felt light on my back as we skidded down to the river. The food did not fit easily into our kayaks, however. We pushed and shoved on it, then found scant room for our legs and feet. But we weren't going far. We pulled upstream around a bend, sweat streaming down our faces, and beached the boats just below the mouth of Dillon Creek.

Dillon Creek Campground, a short distance down the road, would have fresh water, we knew that; and we climbed up to the road with empty water bottles swinging in our hands, our throats woolly with thirst. The water at the campground fountain tasted cold, clean, and free of the iodine we'd grown used to tasting. We filled our quart bottles and drank them to empty, then did it again. When we walked over to a picnic bench, we could hear water sloshing in our bellies. We sat in the shade there and drank more water. I harbored the vague hope that someone would ask us our story and invite us in to a steak feed. Smells of steak wafted maddeningly everywhere, lots of rafting parties laughing and talking around their campfires, some happy Mexican music floating through the pines. We walked the circle of the campground. A few folks waved. We stopped at another empty picnic table and poured water down our throats one more time.

There was a weary, happy feeling in me, a sudden and surprising reversal of the day's earlier frustration. I felt euphoric, in perfect accord with Dev and with myself, with the river and with the sky, felt clean and light and pure as a washed sheet. I felt beaten against rocks, scrubbed, rinsed, bleached by sun, dried by wind. My spirit felt white, fresh, and ready for spreading. We filled our bottles one more time at the fountain, turned and walked back down the road, and down to the river, to our tarp there, and to the waiting cache.

We hadn't said much, didn't say much more—that typically male way of dodging words, no great need in us to jabber, no great need to put words to the deeds of the day. Let the river do the burbling. We would be quiet, feeling a side-by-side affinity, a shared and pleasant silence, with only the occasional word or phrase passing between us.

"Feels good to walk."

"Yeah."

Down at the tarp we sat cross-legged and feasted, making up crackers and kippers for each other with small gestures of care, while evening cooled down in the fading light and the hawk-moths blurred by with that quick, cutting sound of their wings. Our next rapids announced itself at the curve above, its boils just receding opposite our tarp, but we looked at it with the distance of tomorrow. I remembered that distance from the guiding days, remembered all those evenings at Marial Lodge on the Rogue, when, after dinner, we'd walk down to have a look at Mule Creek Canyon, and peer from the path into that chasm, seeing it and feeling it as scenery, as spectacle. Then, in the morning, everything would change, the distance gone, people chattering nervously out on the Marial deck, the canyon beckoning, and not just scenery anymore.

The distance of tomorrow. It was a concept-tonic for sleep, a little like slanting light that smoothes on the river surface, reflecting, and goes no deeper. The undercurrents can wait. There is no hurry. The bedrock bottom of things can wait, is going nowhere. The white thunder of the drops can wait. We used to speak that phrase, "white thunder," whenever the river rumbled distantly, or more often we said "tooonder" to sound like Ingmar Johansson. We reduced the rapids' sounds to puffery that way, to unproven boast, and we could wait, at the distance of our jest, to test those sounds.

My sister, Roberta, arrived in Milwaukee and took over the family duties. I flew back to Oregon. I looked in on my mother and updated her on my father's condition. She did not want to talk about it much, never had wanted to talk about my father again after the divorce.

My father, before his stroke, sometimes tried to ask me about my mother, but could never finish his sentence. I'd tell him the only good thing I could think to tell him, "She keeps that anniversary watch beside her chair." A couple of years back, he had planned a trip, first a visit to Roberta up in Edmonton, then a drive down with Roberta to Oregon to visit me. As part of that trip, he had hoped to visit my mother. My mother hadn't liked that idea much. After her stroke, with her speech stumbling and broken, she felt defenseless. She'd gotten an aide at her assisted-living place to write to my father. She'd sent the message that she didn't want to see him.

It did not surprise me, then, that she had little interest in my father's current condition. But I wanted her to know that I might bring him out to Oregon, that I was looking for an assisted-living place he would like. My mother looked out the window at her bird feeder, gathered herself, and managed a clear line.

"Find us a place," she said. "My room," she pointed at her chair. "His room," she pointed upstairs.

Evidently my father in a wheelchair, unable to speak, no longer threatened her. I could see their meeting again, after thirty years of only the occasional formal card. My father would roll forward in his wheelchair, the bad foot in its steel and foam shield propped out ahead of him like a battering ram, stomach tube tucked neatly between the buttons on his shirt, French beret tilted on his head. He'd be babbling and gesturing. Every now and again he'd say, "Sure!" or "Hell, yes!" and keep rolling on forward. And she, she would be doddering there on her walker, shuffling in her loose slippers, white hair bowl-chopped short around her head like a Modoc elder.

The two of them there together, face to face, after all the sweetness of their honeymoon at Lake Geneva, after the hard years in the cold wheat lands of Montana, after the reasonably good years in Rice Lake, and the good-and-bad years in Minneapolis, and the bitter, fighting years in Milwaukee. Their lives had knocked their words out of their mouths, knocked away some of their memories, pushed their necks forward under their heads, and their legs out from under their frail bodies, but there they would be at the end, with what few words remained and what little strength remained to say them. That faltering final meeting of theirs, as I imagined it, brought a hitch to my chest. I hoped it would happen, a final reconciliation, however late, however odd-worded, staggering, and strange.

I flew back again to Milwaukee. Roberta and I moved my father out to Clement Manor in Greenfield, reputed to be a fine nursing home. It was a Catholic nursing home, and my father shared a room with an ailing priest, Father Mike. A Catholic chapel stood just down the hallway. Catholic litanies floated out of the chapel. I thought it bizarre given that my father had once believed in a Catholic conspiracy to take over the world, a belief flamed by the young men he'd lost from his congregation to the Catholic marriage contract, flamed more, I'm sure, by that long-standing English paranoia—Guy Fawkes, Mary the First, the Lopez Affair, and the rest of it. I'd heard my father inveigh against the Catholic Church since my earliest days. I asked if it bothered him being there in a Catholic home. He just laughed and shook his head. It didn't seem to matter to him anymore.

Roberta returned to Edmonton. I spent the evenings sorting through piles of papers in my father's study. I grubbed around uncovering financial documents, finally added things up and saw that my father had saved a modest sum of money but had never earned much on it. Almost half of it was still in his checking account. It looked like I would need to sell his house and consolidate his various assets if I wanted to work out an assisted-living arrangement for him.

One day I rolled my father into a side room of Clement Manor. I turned off the speaker-piped music and handed him a power-of-attorney document to sign. Two nurses stood by to witness the signing. I had talked it through with my father the day before, had discussed with him the finances I would need for an assisted-living facility, and I thought my father had agreed to my plan. He had told me, miming his meaning, that he wanted a place with a pool table.

But at that moment, with the power-of-attorney document in his lap, he thought again about signing it. It's a long, far leap of faith to sign all your affairs over to somebody else, especially when you yourself have been a stubborn, self-directing mule of a man. And there was that house, the first he'd ever owned, having bought it from Mildred's children after her death. He looked at me long and hard. I wasn't going to push anything. "It's up to you," I said. Finally he shrugged, nodded, and let a nurse help him move his hand in signature.

With what instructions I could understand from my father, I started a serious clean-out of the house. It was big, with two stories and a full basement. Every room, save for the rented upstairs apartment, was crammed with stuff. It took some mental steeling to wade into those rooms filled with family history and start sorting, hauling, and tossing. Fortunately West Allis had a lenient trash policy. The crew picked up everything I hauled out into the back alley—broken chairs, broken dishes, food, bottles, boxes of cards and letters, even the tilted and torn pool table that I sawed into pieces with a chain saw. Word spread to the homeless, evidently, because things began disappearing as quickly as I hauled them out, broken glass all over the alley from their diggings and tossings. I almost put a note up on the alley side of the garage: "Come to the door. Save us both some trouble." But I didn't, just went out and gave the collectors some money, instead, for the trouble of picking up the extra junk, and went out with a broom every few days to sweep up the glass.

"I worked for this outfit one year," I told the collectors. "You guys still save up Hilex labels?"

A soon-to-be-wed nephew drove down from Ontario in a rented truck and picked up the refrigerator, a couple of desks, an air conditioner, a few mirrors, the microwave, the upright freezer, the vacuum cleaner. Various relatives of Mildred and friends of my father came and took what they wanted—sewing machine, TV, Christmas decorations, records, movie projector, picture albums, blankets, silverware. Every day for several weeks I stopped at the Salvation Army store with boxes of donations. A St. Vincent de Paul crew came over from Fond du Lac Avenue and hauled away my father's bed, three upholstered chairs, a sofa, a file cabinet, various end tables and lamps, umpteen boxes of miscellaneous, and three closets full of women's clothing—Clara's, Mildred's, and Mae's.

What remained was harder—all those sermons, for example, several boxes of them, all those old books, all those old records of marriages, funerals, baptisms at which my father had officiated. My father's seminary-class picture hung in one hallway, a portrait of my father hung in the living room, and two watercolor portraits of the children, myself and Roberta, hung on another wall. I could hardly bear to look at any of those pictures. I took them down and put them in a closet, delaying decision. There were notebooks of personal poetry, scrapbooks of humor, reading lists. There was a box of clerical collars. When I looked closely at it, I saw that the manufacturer was one "Parsons and Parsons Co., Cleveland, Ohio." Surely my father had laughed about that. And there in the same box lay the bar of gritty soap meant to keep the collars clean and shiny. My father always struggled in the mornings, his hands at his throat, getting those collars in place.

On the dining room table sat the Swiss grape-leaf music box that I remembered from my childhood. I lifted it, and it started to play again those tunes I had forgotten, *Nach dem Hage* and *Echinnt Sunne.*

I read through snatches of other notebooks and found new lists of incidents my father had wanted to include in his memoirs but hadn't gotten around to writing. They were like random pieces of lost puzzles, or like that draw-string purse of old keys I found in a closet, hundreds of ornate keys to no known locks. The names in the notebooks rang distantly in my head as I read them over. Bud Garret and Buck Balou were Oklahoma outlaws. Kid Can was a Minneapolis gangster; my father had tried to link him to a local murder. Beyond that, I couldn't do much with those names, no more than I could do with those old keys.

One note said, "Lee Trammell, the criminal who became a church elder." I knew about Lee Trammell, one of my father's projects as a parole officer. Various hard types paraded through our home when I was a kid, former bank robbers and such. Lee Trammell was one of them. He was slow and southern of speech, the perfect gentleman at Sunday dinner in our dining room. First he became church janitor, then church elder. One winter night the phone jangled in darkness. A few minutes later my father rushed out the door. He returned the next morning with knife slashes on one arm. Lee Trammell had gone on a drunken spree with a butcher knife. I used to envy those parolees the time my father spent with them, the promise he saw in them, the forgiveness he lavished on them.

Boxes and boxes of pictures stood in the closets, some of them watercolors painted by my mother. There were boxes of jewelry, boxes of leather, boxes of leather-working tools, boxes of etching tools, boxes of old buttons, boxes of oddments I could not even recognize, items from the quondam times.

In an oak box on my father's dresser I found a picture of Thomas in a small gold frame—young Thomas, smiling broadly. Also, two pairs of gold cuff links. Also a gold watch. Also a poster from England announcing a church where a visiting preacher, the Reverend Thomas Carey, from Tishomingo, would preach the morning's sermon. Also letters and pictures of family, and a small picture of Addie Long. Also six ivory-handled knives, the silver stained almost black. Also a copy of the 1906 "Call" to Thomas from the First Presbyterian Church of Tishomingo for a salary of "Four Hundred Fifty Dollars per annum." Also a shoehorn, an old bronze belt buckle, a scattering of foreign coins, two gold wedding bands, and a tiny silver thimble. I took out these items one by one, held them, thought about them, and put them back in the oak box.

No, it's not easy to deal with a house like that, a house that holds old memories and emotions. It's like gutting out an animal. You fight the flashings of your nerves. You pause sometimes over a shoe as though you had been turned into stone. One day, after digging through drawers, I gathered up ten travel clocks, wound them tight, and lined them up all ticking in a row, time's paladins. They said what needed saying to me, that all those nests and piles, all those caches of once-useful things, could not slow down the turning wheels for a minute. Nor could my nostalgia do much of anything but impede the work at hand.

I would clean house like that in the mornings. In the afternoons I'd drive out to Clement Manor and tell my father how the cleanup was going, what I had found, ask his advice on what to keep and what to toss. He'd wave his arms around, meaning "Throw it all away!" Sometimes he'd be down in therapy already when I arrived. They were gentle with him down there, respectful, and went along at his pace. They'd jolly him. I'd go down, sit on a mat, and stretch a little myself. He was starting to swallow better. He was starting to use a walker. He could creep down a hallway with someone at his elbow. We'd talk. He'd babble and gesture. I'd interpret, and he'd nod Yes or No.

They did not always get to him on time in bathroom matters. That was a sore point. An aide would come in, my father would babble and gesture, and the aide would say, "I can't understand you, Reverend," and walk out. So I made a holster to hang on his wheelchair, with a red-lettered placard inside that read, "GET ME TO THE BATHROOM!" I told him if he worked on it he could be the fastest draw in Clement Manor. He gave me a puzzled look for a second, then made a little shooting motion with his thumb and forefinger, and went off into peals of laughter.

Back at my father's house I'd worked my way through the various rooms and closets, then on downstairs past the tools and the fishing tackle, to the area I had been dreading—that half a basement filled with rocks. I did not know what to do with them. There were boxes and boxes of rocks, literally a ton or more of rocks, some of them still in the same boxes we'd shipped them in from railroad heads all over Wyoming and Montana, whenever the family car got so filled up with rocks we hardly had room for ourselves. There were boxes of fire opal, Montana agates, Wyoming dendrite agates, Sweetwater agates, petrified woods, petrified sponges, Lake Superior agates, on and on. Most of the boxes were rotten, rocks already spilling out the bottoms.

On shelves along the walls stood stacks of cigar boxes and tobacco cans filled with smaller stones and cut slabs. Those Idaho garnets from Emerald Creek rattled around in a couple of number-ten cans, also moonstones, snowflake obsidians, red obsidians, moss agates, smoky topaz, geodes, tiger's eyes, thundereggs. Then there was all that rock-working equipment—diamond saws, grinders, tumblers, and cabinets filled with wax, glue, and settings. What a pack rat's horde.

As a teenager, when I was angry or discouraged, I'd go down into the basement, duck my head past the clothes bin, pull out some rough agate the size of a grapefruit, twist it tight in the metal vise, turn on the Martin saw with its diamond blade in an oil bath, and cut open the stone. Something would be there inside, some fantastical geode crystals, or patterns of dendrite, or eyes of color. It was an article of faith that something would be there, previously captive and unseen, something ancient, artful, and mysterious.

My father must have found the same attraction in stones, a soothing analogue to the things he held hidden within himself. Ironic how the two of us, my father and myself, at different times of day and night, stood down there in the basement slabbing up agates, polishing jades, never much speaking to each other, or acknowledging the weight of our marginal relationship, but working separately under the spider webs, rescuing beauty from the hard silences of exterior form.

With those recollections and guilts playing in me, it did not seem right to simply throw all those stones away, all those boxes, those semi-precious pounds. One night I actually began carrying boxes up from the basement and out to the Buick. It was midnight, raining. I thought I'd cruise around to the parks and the playgrounds of West Allis and put out agates and Eden Valley woods like Easter eggs. I'd put them out in places where children could find them. They could start up their own basement caches, I thought. But finally I paused and realized that I'd probably get arrested for my trouble.

In the end I kept out a few special pieces, then called a rock shop owner in Sheboygan. He drove down with a big truck, poked through the stuff, made me an offer, and hauled it all away.

⇆

On the Klamath that night, down on the bar below Dillon Creek, Dev and I made ready for sleeping. Neither of us could face another sweltering night inside a sleeping bag. We lay down on top of the bags. To ward off mosquitoes, we wrapped ourselves in what clothes we had. I pulled my wind jacket around my feet, wrapped my wind pants around my neck and face. I looked up at the darkening sky through a thin gap in the wind pants. Mosquitoes danced there, buzzing and hovering. I felt comfortable enough, pretty well protected from mosquitoes and not too hot.

"This is working," I said.

"We should have thought of this sooner."

We lay there watching the stars come out. I felt a lot better than I had felt down in the Canyon of the Ikes, still pretty tired, but mentally better. My stomach was filled with crackers and kippers. I'd had all the fresh water I could drink. I felt close to Dev and happy with this confluence place. The mosquitoes were at bay. The air was clean, the smells fresh, the chirping of the crickets musical and reassuring. The rapids above us at the bend rumbled, but it wasn't really much of a rapids. I knew that from past seasons and past runs. Anyway, it was not yet time to test those sounds. They could wait. They could pass for lullaby until the morning.

Inland Ocean

The real river flows under the river.

—James Galvin

In the canyon above Dillon Creek several rafting parties whooped their ways past us as we paddled. The road ran close beside the channel, with support rigs rattling up and down, some empty, some hauling kayaks and rafts. The river held a series of closely spaced rapids, more than we remembered from years of higher water. None of the rapids were big, but the current against us ran constant, with few upstream eddies. We made slow progress. It was hot. My mind trudged along counting river words in time to my paddling—*river left, river right, upriver, downriver, riverine, river rat, riverbed, riverside, river bottom, riverscape.* At *old man river* my mind turned to working songs, those with a steady lift and pull.

Noonish we beached the kayaks. Our felts flapped on the stones as we walked, and we lifted our feet high to keep from tripping. Behind a low bush, we took what shade we could manage. The gravel bar around us shimmered with heat waves. Runny peanut butter and broken crackers were all we had left in the way of lunch food. We'd gotten practiced at eating that fare with our river knives. As we sat there licking at goop, a single kayaker pivoted neatly out of the current into the eddy in front of us.

I said, "Is that you, Dave? Dave Payne?"

"That's me, "he said.

We had worked with Dave, a kayaking ranger, in commercial matters—boat ID, special regulations, camping permits. He squinted into the shade. "Who's that?"

I told him our names. He squinted some more and said, "Sure. Hi there. It's been awhile."

"Looks like a lot of traffic on this section," I said.

"That's right. Low water makes it a good run."

Dev and I didn't mention what we were doing. We still had no camping permit. Payne sculled idly with his paddle while we talked. His presence reminded me of all those conventions of downstream form, all those regulations, all those people stacked up at the put-ins and the take-outs; and it hit me how Dev and I had left real solitude down in Kenek Canyon, how we had labored diligently to get past the best part of the Klamath and on up to the crowded, accessible section, and for no other reason than our insistence on getting somewhere. It might be good to leave again from Requa and stop at Blue Creek or Kenek Canyon for a month, or a year.

Payne asked how we'd been keeping, asked if we had any boat problems, then said goodbye and pushed off down the river, checking his territory, doing his job. Dev and I climbed back into our own kayaks and paddled a few more upstream miles.

At Ukonom Creek we pulled in at a standard camping spot just upstream of the creek's mouth. We hadn't made many miles for the day, but the slow mood of the shady bush held in our minds. We wanted to find some place to cool down. Also, we had good memories of Ukonom Creek, of the trail up to the falls and the people we'd taken there, and of the big surfing wave down below, last play-spot before the standard take-out at Coon Creek.

We spread the tarp, set up camp, tied off the kayaks, and walked back down to the river, the sand hot between our toes. A couple of small eddies circled lazily next to shore. We jumped in there and bobbed around. When we had cooled, we scrubbed our shirts with sand, rinsed them, and draped them on stones to dry. A line from the *Pentateuch* reads: "The odor of my son is like that of a field blessed by the Lord." That's true enough, and true beyond the sweet smells of baby breath and baby powder. It's true under the hot sun. Nevertheless, the river bath was a good idea for us both, and the washing out of shirts.

We had the place to ourselves, nobody dropping down through Machine Rapids and the deep canyon below that to the Ukonom sandbar, much as I thought somebody might. We boiled pasta, poured some freeze-dried corn over the top of it, and garnished the whole affair with pepper. It tasted fine. We washed our dishes with sand. Light and time were with us, a hit-and-miss luxury. We sat cross-legged on the tarp and played another game of go.

Dev explained how he described commonplace things in go terminology—river rapids, for example. Also, he'd structured his Ph.D. dissertation so that he could move in any of several directions as things developed, a standard strategy of go. He could see the patterns and the possibilities. He instructed me to do the same, to see both the details and the larger structures, both the near and the far. I liked that idea but found it hard to implement. Caught up with the plight of this piece and that piece, I lost track of bigger things.

"Pull back a little," Dev said. "Let your eyelids droop. Take in the patterns."

I tried that. The wall extending down the left side of the board was six unique pieces, but also it was a journey. It was stasis, but it was movement. That piece was an "I," but the grouping was a "Thou." Maybe this probing into fathers, too, was an encompassing, a seeing of near and far, seeing Oklahoma Territory and Weitchpec as related places of the world, getting Consett, Scott City, Tishomingo, and Milwaukee into the film of one eyeball, getting the Washita, the Peace, and the Klamath into one single mind's canyon, near and far, holding still and moving on.

I kept losing at go, but it did not matter. With darkness settling, we dropped the pennies back into their bag, rolled up the board. We made rudimentary talk, such as it is with us, but talk that had passed beyond the tensions of Ishi Pishi into a slower, more harmonic run.

"The Winston man," said Dev.

"Mr. K," I said.

We laughed remembering that trip, a promotional trip for Mr. K's river gear, the Winston cigarette model brought along for posed shots. However, it was Mr. K's photograph that ended up on the boxes. I'd seen those photos in the sterile landscapes of WalMart and BiMart—Mr. K in Machine Rapids with his paddle raised uselessly high, spray flying, Mr. K, the chunky Russian wheeler-dealer.

Toward the end of that trip, walking with Mr. K down the shoreline of Little Blossom, checking the angle for photographs, I'd asked him about his origins. He'd said nothing and kept walking. We'd reached that big boulder dividing the river. I thought he'd ignored the question, or had not heard it. I let it go. Suddenly he turned to me. He said, "My father was a Nazi collaborator. We fled Russia after the war. I haven't seen my father, or written to my father, in thirty years."

Dev, recalling that same trip, said, "The Winston Man was a pretty nice guy, actually."

"Yeah, he was."

"Good in his boat. Not too cocky. Pleasant in camp."

"Yup," I said, and we went silent for awhile remembering that odd trip.

Dev switched to other nostalgias. "I brought most of my best friends down here to Ukonom. Including my girlfriends—Christie, Joan, Mary."

I added a memory of my own. "There used to be an old teepee just around the bend upstream; this was when I first started running the Klamath. Hasn't been there for some years now. It was deep in the bushes and hard to see unless you turned upstream."

"Upstream," Dev said, and we both smiled.

"I always looked, but never saw anybody around the place. It was gone by the time you started coming down here."

We went on like that for awhile. Finally we edged around to the topic of our trip. My expectations had receded from the grand adventure. I was paring them down to realistic proportion. Dev, for his part, said he was finding values in the pools of the river, where, often as not, he waited for me to catch up.

He said, "I like the still water. There are more frogs there, and more bugs to watch."

That admission didn't much surprise me, knowing Dev, and it was lucky he could find those quieter values of the pools, because the values of heroic sojourn were getting away from us. Ideally, for an expedition-scale, upstream marathon, Dev should have found a partner better matched to his youthful stamina. He thought he had, of course, fooled by memory and that chimera of the invincible father. I thought he had, too, fooled by other things, fooled by stubbornness.

For the last two days I had been thinking about Irongate Reservoir on the Oregon border as a more realistic destination. But even Irongate was looking a very long way off. If I could have wished myself up the remaining miles to Klamath Marsh, to Petskuk, the Inland Ocean, I would have done that; I would have made it there neck-and-neck with Upstream Coyote, getting wiser by the mile. But the tied-to-flesh part of myself, the part that held down the tarp in a wind, was probably not going to make it a whole lot farther up the Klamath. I knew that in the deep recesses of my muscles and in the marrow of my bones.

As twilight settled across the canyon, Dev and I talked further. We had already come far enough to "keep our pride," as Dev put it. Actually, he had first made that observation seventy miles back down the river, under the Weitchpec Bridge. The important thing from Ukonom on up, we agreed, was state of mind.

Dev said, "I want to hear the music."

We were both intrigued by the long, slow canyon bend above Happy Camp, having never run it. We had always considered it too slow for the downstream mode. We used to joke about that stretch, calling it "very pleasant water." But thinking about it on Ukonom beach, we looked forward to exploring its pools and crannies. We didn't want to spoil it by pushing through too quickly.

It was that thought that swayed us to aim for a take-out at Thompson Creek. We'd still need to get up past most of the rapids drawn on the cover of my journal—The Dragon's Tooth, Osprey, Change-of-Course, Trench, Pre-Trench, Mixmaster, The Devil's Toenail (that last one a circus on every trip I'd ever run, swimmers everywhere, bags and paddles floating away down the river), and then on up through Kanaka with its keeper-hole and its stories, on up past Happy Camp where we could stop in for some supplies, then on into that deep, quiet canyon of slow water. Upstream from that canyon it wasn't far to Thompson Creek, with only a few more steep drops, and that good play-wave at Seattle Creek. We calculated it would all take about eight more days of paddling. I thought I could manage eight more days.

We lay on the tarp talking and looking at stars. Dev pointed out some constellations I did not know, Cepheus and Boötes. He told me about his bike trip through Montana with his friend Jack, how they got caught in a snowstorm on Chief Joseph Pass, how they got locked in the women's dorm of the state college at Dillon, how they rode the rails back to Portland, freezing in rain on a flatcar.

He told me about Paonia, Colorado, and his teaching there. I was glad he felt free to share it all.

We looked up at Draco. It made a sinuous curvature through the sky. Remarkably, the curves of Draco resembled the course of the Klamath River. If you placed Eltanin, the brightest star in Draco's head, over Dad's Camp at the Klamath's mouth, you could match the two courses upstream through the sky, the river and the dragon's tail swooping and twisting in synchrony. Crickets chirped as we figured it, as though to say, "See, see, see."

Draco's path amounted to a fine cosmic affirmation, but before I could get too overweening about it all, a cautionary thought flitted out of my brain. I recalled a scribbled notation in the *New Testament and Psalms* of Thomas. That Testament (inscribed "Thos. Carey, Tishomingo, 1909") had literally fallen apart in my hands when I'd first picked it up in my father's study. I had stored it in a zippered plastic bag and did not touch it for some time. One day I took it out, and it fell open to Matthew 7.13: "Enter ye in by the narrow gate: for wide is the gate, and broad is the way, that leadeth to destruction, and many are they that enter in thereby."

Thomas's marginalia on this passage, as best I could make it out, read as follows:

> *The Straight gate and Narrow way = only way for us.*
> *Resistance. Rocks = Snags. God's Sculpture.*
> *This path = strongest character. Tall and grand because*
> *narrow and deep. No joy so sweet as found in resistance.*

There in the sand of Ukonom, almost one hundred hard miles from the Pacific, I finally saw those words for what they were— fourteen-karat upstream sentiments. I started at the realization, not sure just where to go with it, except to see, once more, that it's no easy thing to escape the fathers. You take the twenty-two off the wall, and set off down the railroad tracks, but sooner or later some old-boy sheriff finds you and brings you back to where you began.

Dev and I shared a lot together—stories, places, the curvings of Draco; but we shared, too, our idea of the upstream mode, and shared it with Thomas, a notion of the hard path, a notion that passed down through God-knows-what twists and permutations on its way from the Territory to the water-worn, stony road of the Klamath River. No more fitting place to make that realization, either, than where Ukonom Creek washed wild and clear down a long slope of the Marble Mountains to where its last icy burble into the Klamath chilled the big river for half a mile downstream, and where, when you waded across the creek on the way up to the falls, its cold reached up around your feet and squeezed them numb.

↜

My father underwent surgery on his bad foot. He lay in pre-op with a blue net over the top of his head. After the surgery, he lay in post-op with terrible leg cramps. I had sometimes wondered if my father was as tough as he'd claimed. Watching him bulldog his way through that suffering, I decided he was. It appeared he was going to make it through these complications on sheer stubbornness, and in my heart I applauded him. I never bought the belief, evident among some younger doctors, that at eighty-seven it is one's duty to die quickly and clear a bed in the ward. Power to him, I thought, for as long as he wants to stay around.

I had hopes for him. To be accepted into an assisted-living unit, he had to get to where he could swallow solids and feed himself. Also, to satisfy fire regulations, he had to be able to walk down a hallway with his walker. If he could do those two things, he could have an apartment with food service and laundry service provided, and with that pool table in the rec room. There would be plenty of company for him in that kind of place, plenty of partners for the pool games, plenty of audience for his ready jokes. He had a ways yet to go in therapy, but I believed he would make it.

I kept cleaning out the house until it was sufficiently empty to get at the walls and the floors. I called in the Merry Maids, and they arrived at the doorstep one morning in little skirts and hats, their workboxes filled with rags and spray cans. I had chosen a real-estate agent by then, and we had set a price. She showed the house a few times. Two weeks later I walked into Clement Manor and gave my father the news—the house was sold.

It upset him. He started waving and babbling.

"Wait a minute," I said, wondering if I had overstepped myself. "We talked this all over, remember? I'd sell the house so we'd have the funds to get you into an assisted-living place."

He paused for a minute, then nodded and tapped his head. He'd forgotten.

"We're set now," I said. "All I need to do is find you the perfect place. All you need to do is get so you can swallow and walk a little better."

He worked on a word for awhile. "Much," he said.

"How much?"

He nodded, yes, and I told him. He seemed satisfied with the price. Until that house, he'd lived his life in church manses. That house had been his own place. He'd put a lot of labor into its walls, ceilings, fences, windows, drainpipes. It was tangible home ground. I had thought hard about just keeping it as a psychological prop for him, so he'd know his things were there, know the memories were there, if he could get well enough to return. But it would take live-in care for that to work. He had no one in Milwaukee to give him that, and he couldn't afford to hire it.

"There's a beautiful new assisted-living place out in Hales Corners," I told him. "I've gone through it all and gotten preliminary approvals. It's clean and nice. There's a pool table. Or you can come out to Oregon. There are a couple places out there I want to check out. Then you can decide."

He nodded. He said he was sorry he'd left me such a mess in the house. He was glad to have all those clothes and boxes gone. He'd have done it himself if he could have found the energy. He said this in the language we had worked out together, filled with nods and gestures, a partial language, but adequate.

By this time it was late fall. The days were crisp. I had to get back to Oregon. But I felt energized by the action of rescue, confident that my father would swallow again, walk again, however haltingly. I felt confident that the therapy would speed him toward recovery, that other parts of his brain would take over, grow, and connect, that things would all come together for him. I'd find a place for him near my home in Oregon, if not with a pool table, then I'd buy a pool table for our own basement and bring him over to shoot eight-ball, or I'd find that place where both he and my mother could live. I thought we would have a few last years of accord.

The day before I left, he asked me to take him outside. I helped him get on his sweatpants, his shirt, a big white cardigan, put on his beret, wrapped a checkered scarf around his neck, got him into his wheelchair, threw a blanket over his lap, and rolled him outside into the sunshine. Mums were blooming beside an apartment complex across from the back parking lot. A few mare's-tail clouds floated in the sky. A wind kicked dead leaves down a bank of grass and whirled them around in circles across the asphalt. My father circled his hand. I stopped the wheelchair. He looked up at the sky and across at the whirling leaves. He looked at them for a long time. Even then, with all my hopes and plans, I sensed the farewell in it.

Back inside again, we sat for a time before I got him into his bed. I held his hand and told him to work hard in therapy. I told him I'd be back to see him right after Christmas. He smiled and nodded. When I got up to leave, he pulled back my hand with his one good arm. He pulled me down close. I bent my head to kiss his cheek, but he pulled me down further, and he kissed me on the lips.

⇐

Dev and I were up before sunrise. After some granola, we paddled off up the canyon into that diffused glow of first light. I worried about some canyon twists I remembered, some shifty places not far above Ukonom, but they proved easy, with boulders to dodge behind, and eddies to work. We paddled the north side of Machine Rapids without any problems. There was a slack feeling in my muscles, but my mind felt good.

We powered our way up a section of stiff currents and jumped a couple of chutes. It was all going fast and smooth. If I'd been tuned properly to the ancestors, I might have remembered about pride and destruction. Suddenly I was upside-down and wedged between stones. Churning bubbles blinded me. My paddle-sweep hit the unyielding face of stone, once, and then again. My attempts to pry upright didn't work. I panicked, pulled loose the spray-skirt, and bailed out.

It took us awhile, then, to get the kayak to shore and emptied. I kept snorting and hacking. My sinuses felt like they'd been reamed out with a sewer snake. Those bubbles still danced around my eyes, and my arms still felt the confining thuds of my paddle-blade against stone. Dev remained unworried, not bothered by the delay. He was feeling good about our talk at Ukonom.

I pulled myself together enough to keep paddling, and we worked on up to the Dragon's Tooth, carried over the drop there, and pulled over beside a rafting party still scouting the rapids. From them we begged a roll of duct tape, a small roll, only enough for a couple of wraps around the felts. The wraps came loose again within the hour. We passed more gold dredges, paddled around their anchor lines and through the unnatural currents of gouged channels. The whole day had turned over for me. Everything looked skewered, flipped, off-center.

Part way into the afternoon, as I opted to shore-hug a route up a rapids, Dev paddled over to me and said, "You can tell me to go to hell if you want to, but why don't you just get out into the whitewater?"

My river confidence at that moment was at an all-time low. I was shaky. I was getting paranoid about my sinuses, not wanting anymore water rammed down my nostrils. My kayak kept shipping water, wallowing, and making more cracking noises. I thought it was close to breaking open. About then my resolve developed some cracks of its own. The only thing driving me forward at that point was Dev and his hope to make Thompson Creek, but I realized I was going to disappoint Dev in other ways by staying on the river. With the kayak breaking, the felts flopping, and my reserves scraping bottom, it didn't make much sense for me to keep going.

Maybe it was all the weight I was losing, shedding over two pounds a day, as it worked out, always an enervating process. To leaven my spirits a little I recalled that somewhere in these parts, during the mining days, when pork was a prized commodity, one Amanda Roberts had kept a hog weighing over five hundred pounds. That hog was so fat it could hardly waddle. Its eyes were so squeezed shut by fat that it couldn't see. I shaped that beast out in my imagination. Its specter cast a humongous shadow across the landscape that only made mine seem the more diminished.

"I'm going to take out at Independence Bridge," I said. The words popped out of my mouth almost without volition, but once I'd said them, the intention felt deep and needful. "I just don't belong on this river in my present shape."

Dev frowned. "Let's camp here if you're tired," he said. "Think about it overnight, at least."

"No," I said. "No, I'm taking out."

It felt like I had caught the trough of a surfing wave, and it held me. I had my paddle out into the lift of the wave, braced and solid and staying there. We were down around Osprey Rapids at the time, an osprey nest in the tree above it year after year. The river poured under me, complex emotions poured through me.

I remembered how close I had felt to my father in those last days when he needed my help. But he hadn't liked it much. He'd accepted his limitations, but had no tolerance for any altered definition of himself. Some of his closest friends had come to visit him one day at Clement Manor, and when they had gone, he'd waved an angry and despairing hand of dismissal after them, friends of half a lifetime. He didn't want sympathy. He was sick of sympathy. Find him some place, he told me, where he could make new friends with people in wheelchairs, people like himself. Self-definition keeps shop all hours, and what was true with my father was true with me. I was still guide enough, and stubborn father enough, too, to take myself off the river when that seemed to me like the best decision.

Dev and I paddled in charged silence from Osprey up to Independence Bridge, got out there, and sat down in the sand. Tears welled up in my eyes, and I could not hold them. Tears of failure, of exhaustion, of frustration, I'm not sure which. Dev's own tears spilled over and ran down his cheeks. Our dream had deflated, our bubble had bursted, our aspirations had collapsed and washed back down the long way we had come.

                          ↝

Up on the road above the bridge two women in a pickup let me hop in the back of their rig. I hunkered there with about a hundred rolling Pepsi cans, a few thousand cigarette butts, and some remnant chicken feed. They stopped at Clear Creek when I rapped on the cab window.

"We'll take you on into Happy Camp if you want," said the driver.

But I'd seen that red phone box I'd been looking for, right by the side of the bridge, and figured it would do. After I'd jumped out, though, and after they'd pulled away, I found the phone had no coin-slots. I had to dial my friend collect. Wes said he had a class to teach the following morning, but could leave by noon, get down there sometime in middle afternoon. I said that would be fine.

The sun was dropping away. A couple of woodpeckers dipped across a clearing to the east. I had a thumb in the air when another pickup rounded the corner, headed back toward Independence Bridge. The pickup pulled over, no handle on the door. Within a few minutes the chisel-faced, bib-overalled old-timer at the wheel was telling me that the wealth of the world was buried away in catacombs beneath the streets of Rome. He said Rome was just another name for Babylon, mother of harlots, and that the Pope and George Bush had ruined the world some years back, stolen everything the people had and buried it in the catacombs.

"You heard him yerself, I'll bet. 'Third World,' he said."

I said I hadn't. I was looking out the window at what pieces of the Klamath I could see through the pines, thinking what a beautiful river it was, feeling its eddies and currents again, feeling all those emotions I had invested in it.

When we reached Independence Bridge, the old tub-thumper had worked his diatribe on past the mark of the beast to local jobs. I was pleased to affirm something, by way of thanks.

"The area certainly could use a few jobs," I said.

I climbed out. He threw me a thin smile, eased back on the clutch, and rattled off down the road. I walked down the path to the river. Dev still sat on the ground where I'd left him, still with his lifejacket on. He kept throwing stones out into the water.

I thought again of that time on the Umpqua when Dev was young and in tears, and I was saying, no, we walk this rapids with this borrowed canoe, invoking that old parental stance of authority and judgment. There on that Klamath riverbank, watching Dev pegging stones, I was in control again, as on the Umpqua, making the judgments again, and still doing it like the stereotypical, have-to-be-right father.

It's a long river pull, I guess, to the place we'd like to be in ourselves, if we even know where that is. I knew I hadn't gotten there. Dev and I had shared the bruises, the blisters, the hunger, the hard gains, but this last judgment I had made alone. It felt as though I had leveraged some unfair advantage, as though I had reached out and grabbed the old bully-stick of paternity.

Dev looked over at me as I squatted down beside him. He said he'd settled it in his mind. It was all right. It was a decision he could accept. But the air stayed thick with feelings. We pulled the kayaks high up the shore, laid out the tarp one last time, and opened some kippers. We ate kippers and looked across the darkening river at the orange cables and yellow pumps of the gold dredges anchored cross-stream. We looked at Independence Creek braiding steeply down through the gravels of the far shore. A gust of wind blew over the river and across the beach. It raised a dry and bitter dustiness to our nostrils.

Our scabbed and battered legs lined out in front of us on the tarp. I looked at them. At least we're blooded, I thought, smeared with cabalistic upstream sign. At least we've traveled some of the hard road. But I wished it could have been better, a better ending, something more than just stopping at the bridge. We had come too far, worked too hard, and shared too much, to feel so close to failure.

"I want it to be good between us," I said.

"Me too," Dev said.

Our hands came together in an affirming clasp. We held that clasp, hard and strong, for a long time. I sensed the fathers there with us, in all their hard postures, but with something softer in their expressions. And I realized that life blood and the regeneration of things were not simply the purview of that Inland Ocean up at Petskuk, that place where we'd been headed. People had crawled out of the earth all along this river, down there at those world centers, at Sugarloaf Mountain, at the confluence of the Trinity. There was that stone altar on the beach up at Clear Creek where the Karoks held ceremonies each spring for the renewal of the world. There were tiny hop-toads on every beach. There was Sweet William's frog pond. There were a hundred-odd other pools where Dev had watched frogs and bugs. A place of origins could be small like that, and smell like minnows. It could be as vast as a marsh, or as tiny as a seed. It might fit the circle of one windblown blade of grass. It might cup at the center of clasped hands. The river comes down from Petskuk as connection, as a reaching out of lake to sea, of fresh water to salt water, one long synergy of insistence, one continuous flowing of forms (eddy and riffle, merganser and eel), one pouring idea of regeneration and renewal. We had tapped into some of that connection at least. I knew it with the strength of our arms, and with the firm intertwine of our fingers. Out of all our own craziness, and out of all the craziness in the world, we had found that much sanity.

Dev and I unrolled our sleeping bags. We lay on our backs, looking up at the stars as they came out, and waited for sleep to come. Some animal crashed once in the bushes behind us. The last bird-songs and cricket-chirps faded away. We lay there on our blue tarp, aware of its boundaries, choosing its boundaries, held close by its boundaries.